Egypt After the Spring:
Revolt and Reaction

Edited by Emile Hokayem

with Hebatalla Taha

Egypt After the Spring:
Revolt and Reaction

Edited by Emile Hokayem

with Hebatalla Taha

IISS The International Institute for Strategic Studies

The International Institute for Strategic Studies

Arundel House | 13–15 Arundel Street | Temple Place | London | WC2R 3DX | UK

First published January 2016 **Routledge**
4 Park Square, Milton Park, Abingdon, Oxon, OX14 4RN

for **The International Institute for Strategic Studies**
Arundel House, 13–15 Arundel Street, Temple Place, London, WC2R 3DX, UK
www.iiss.org

Simultaneously published in the USA and Canada by **Routledge**
270 Madison Ave., New York, NY 10016

Routledge is an imprint of Taylor & Francis, an Informa Business

DIRECTOR-GENERAL AND CHIEF EXECUTIVE Dr John Chipman
EDITOR Dr Nicholas Redman
EDITORIAL MANAGER Nancy Turner
ASSISTANT EDITOR James Middleton
EDITORIAL Alice Aveson, Jill Lally, Chris Raggett
COVER/PRODUCTION John Buck, Kelly Verity
COVER IMAGES iStockphoto/Joel Carillet/Karim Mostafa; USMC/Matt Epright; USAF/
Myles Cullen; Kremlin.ru; Wilson Dias/ABr; World Economic Forum

The International Institute for Strategic Studies is an independent centre for research, information and debate on the problems of conflict, however caused, that have, or potentially have, an important military content. The Council and Staff of the Institute are international and its membership is drawn from almost 100 countries. The Institute is independent and it alone decides what activities to conduct. It owes no allegiance to any government, any group of governments or any political or other organisation. The IISS stresses rigorous research with a forward-looking policy orientation and places particular emphasis on bringing new perspectives to the strategic debate.

The Institute's publications are designed to meet the needs of a wider audience than its own membership and are available on subscription, by mail order and in good bookshops. Further details at www.iiss.org.

Printed and bound in Great Britain by Bell & Bain Ltd, Thornliebank, Glasgow

British Library Cataloguing in Publication Data
A catalogue record for this book is available from the British Library

Library of Congress Cataloging in Publication Data

ADELPHI series
ISSN 1944-5571

ADELPHI 453–454
ISBN 978-1-138-65342-9

Contents

ACKNOWLEDGEMENTS

I first want to thank all nine authors for their excellent contributions to this *Adelphi* volume. I am delighted that this group includes some of the top scholars of Egypt alongside some of the best rising analysts of the country.

I wish to thank Nick Redman, editor of the *Adelphi* series, for his guidance and patience before and throughout the editorial process; Nancy Turner for her assistance; John Buck for designing the cover; and James Middleton for his editorial assistance.

In addition to authoring a chapter, Heba Taha served as an extremely able, pleasant and sharp partner.

Islam El-Tayeb made an essential contribution to the conceptualisation and commissioning of this volume.

I thank Sir John Jenkins, who as Executive Director of the IISS–Middle East since January 2015 inherited this research project among others, for his support and intellectual input.

Emile Hokayem

CONTRIBUTORS

Emile Hokayem is the Senior Fellow for Middle East Security at the International Institute for Strategic Studies based out of its Middle East office in Manama, Bahrain. He is the author of *Syria's Uprising and the Fracturing of the Levant*, published by the IISS and Routledge in June 2013, and the co-editor of *Middle Eastern Security, the US Pivot and the Rise of ISIS*, published by the IISS and Routledge in January 2015.

Professor Nathan J. Brown is Professor of Political Science and International Affairs at George Washington University and non-resident senior associate at the Carnegie Endowment for International Peace.

Professor Ellis Goldberg is Professor Emeritus of Political Science at the University of Washington in Seattle. He has published numerous articles and books on the political economy of twentieth-century Egypt. He has taught at Harvard, Princeton and the American University in Cairo, and has been a Carnegie Scholar and a Guggenheim Fellow.

Dr Zeinab Abul-Magd is Associate Professor of Middle Eastern History at Oberlin College, US, and the author of *Militarizing the Nation: Army, Business, and Revolution in Egypt, 1952–2015* (New York: Columbia University Press, forthcoming in 2016).

Yasser El-Shimy is a doctoral candidate at Boston University's Department of Political Science. He worked as the International Crisis Group's Egypt analyst (2011–13) and as a Middle East research fellow at the Harvard Kennedy School's Middle East Initiative (2014–15).

Michael Wahid Hanna is a senior fellow at The Century Foundation and an adjunct senior fellow at the Center on Law and Security at New York University School of Law. He works on issues of international security, international law, and US foreign policy in the Middle East and South Asia.

Dr H.A. Hellyer is a non-resident senior fellow at the Atlantic Council, and an Associate Fellow in International Security Studies at the Royal United Services Institute in London. A widely published commentator and analyst, his book on the Egyptian uprising is due to be published in mid-2016 by Hurst and Oxford University Press.

Gamal Hassan is an independent Egyptian author who specialises in Middle East politics and Egypt's foreign policy. He contributes a weekly column for the leading Egyptian daily *Al-Masry Al-Youm* and his articles appear in various publications, including the leading pan-Arab daily *Al-Shark Al-Awsat*.

Hebatalla Taha is a research analyst at the International Institute for Strategic Studies and a D.Phil candidate at St Antony's College, University of Oxford.

Mohamed El Dahshan is a development economist, working with governments and international organisations to advise on sectoral growth policies. He is also the founder of Heliopolis Consulting, and a Fellow with the Tahrir Institute for Middle East Policy. He is a frequent contributor to international media.

INTRODUCTION

Emile Hokayem

The revolution in Egypt in 2011 opened an exceptionally tumultuous and contentious chapter of the country's history. Where
the journey towards democracy and dignity – the apparent
aspirations of Egyptians who participated in the uprising
– went awry is difficult to pin down. Indeed, what followed
the stunning resignation of Hosni Mubarak in February of
that year remains unclear and is disputed by many, even as
President Abdel Fattah Al-Sisi attempts to further consolidate
his authority.

Constantly changing transitional road maps; complex
calculations and changing alignments of political, revolutionary and other forces; shifting preferences of the population;
fluctuating levels of street politics; and competing interests
of state institutions have made for dizzying, uncertain and at
times debilitating politics. This has affected Egypt's regional
role. Size, history and geography make it a giant of the
modern Middle East. However, as it faces internal upheaval
and reordering, it appears to be culturally and economically
dormant and to have retreated from its role as a dominant
power.

Political scientist Marc Lynch applied a powerful analytical tool to study Egyptian dynamics: Calvinball, 'a game defined by the absence of rules – or, rather, that the rules are made up as they go along'.[1] In the Egyptian context, Calvinball meant that the parameters, pace and trajectory of the apparent transition were never fully set, creating decisive uncertainty for all political actors and observers. Yet perhaps unsurprisingly, such bewildering dynamics have produced the most probable of all outcomes: a reassertion of a military-dominated autocracy and popular quiescence.

During this period, observers and Egyptians have argued over what has really been happening, who is in charge, what interests have been pursued and what mistakes have been made. To this day, the exit of Mubarak is alternatively described as the outcome of a popular revolution, a soft military coup to preserve the system, or even as an act of personal magnanimity.

The ousting in 2013 of Muhammad Morsi, the Muslim Brotherhood leader who served briefly as Egypt's first civilian president, is a matter of even greater controversy. Was it a popular revolution in protest at his performance and Islamist agenda or a military coup that shaped and exploited undeniable popular dissatisfaction? Complicating analysis is that each of these interpretations carries some degree of validity: they are often not mutually exclusive, and therefore allow competing narratives to gain credence. It is no surprise, then, that levels of polarisation in Egyptian society are at an all-time high and are having a profound societal impact.

Political developments between these extraordinary events were equally confusing. Political and state actors competed for power and relevance, but mutable frameworks and rules, as well as imbalances in organisation and cohesion, created an uneven field. Various factions proclaimed themselves guardians of the revolution – even counter-revolutionary forces, in an attempt to co-opt and hijack the transformation – but rarely agreed on what had been achieved, what needed to be preserved and what more needed to be done. What ensued was political cacophony and a sense of disorder, something not lost on the many Egyptian citizens who, above all else, craved order.

This period was filled with ironies and reversals. Following the apparently irresistible rise of political Islamism in 2012, the Brotherhood faced a momentous setback within a year. Once in office, Islamists who had professed adherence to democratic pluralism and processes quickly monopolised power and alienated factions that had, however reluctantly, supported their rise. In response, secularists, who had decried political exclusion and state violence in 2011, began to rationalise and justify mass repression of the Islamists. Many Egyptian people, who in 2011 appeared steadfast in their defence of new freedoms and political diversity, accepted and even supported the return of the military to the public arena by 2013.

Amid the dizzying politics, some things have remained constant. The resilience of the Egyptian state during this turmoil has been remarkable but unsurprising. A high degree of institutionalisation meant that the state could weather the upheaval – in contrast with Libya and Syria – but also that attempts at genuine reform faced built-in, systemic resistance. As with many uprisings, revolutionary fervour eventually spent itself against entrenched, well-organised and adaptable remnants of the regime, but also popular fatigue and apathy.

Also to be anticipated was the centrality of the military in politics. If at times it stood in the background, it was decisive at key junctures, steering the transition, mollifying, constraining and bringing down the Brotherhood and other political forces, and finally assuming power. Likewise, foreign policy has remained consistent throughout this period.

It is difficult to clearly isolate and quantify the costs of four years of upheaval. Regardless of who is responsible, Egypt's long-standing economic and social ills have certainly been amplified. Public disillusionment has compounded the wishful and negligent policymaking that led to the 2011 uprising. Political expediency and the use of public resources to shore up the ruling elite have complicated strategies to reform the economy.

There are other costs. As Sisi consolidates his authority, Egypt is facing its most severe Islamist insurgency. This is partly a consequence of radicalisation since 2013 but also because of exogenous factors that thrive on domestic discontent.

This *Adelphi* volume attempts to make sense of these dynamics, shed light on the period between 2011 and 2015 and determine the factors that will shape Egypt's trajectory under Sisi. It provides a rigorous and comprehensive assessment of every aspect of contemporary politics and policy, insights about the workings of society and government, and indications about what lies ahead for the country.

The first three chapters deal with the frameworks and institutions of the state. Nathan J. Brown revisits the various transition plans put in place in 2011 and explains how their designs and flaws influenced the various outcomes. His chapter details some of the fundamental paradoxes encapsulated in the revolution and the transition.

Ellis Goldberg provides an in-depth analysis of two of the state's core institutions: the security forces and the judiciary. He illustrates how they have inserted themselves into the politics of the transition to secure their interests.

The third chapter, by Zeinab Abul-Magd, turns to the core of the Egyptian state, the military, and sheds light on its complex involvement in the country's economy and politics. She shows how the military has continuously adapted to the different stages since 2011, and reveals the extent of its institutionalisation, and how deeply it has penetrated the state.

Building on this discussion of the state, the next three chapters deal with the key political actors that emerged in the aftermath of 2011. Yasser El-Shimy looks into the thinking and behaviour of the Brotherhood throughout the transition period. He explains how within the space of a year the Islamist organisation went from dominating Egypt to being banned and falling into disarray.

Michael Wahid Hanna analyses the disparate array of non-Islamist political forces that have struggled to position themselves and ensure their relevance to the ever-changing politics. He discusses several stages of fracture within non-Islamist parties, which have ultimately led to the demise of a genuine political opposition.

H.A. Hellyer looks at the role of civil-society groups in the political transformation, and their often painful adjustment to less-than-satisfactory outcomes. He details the role of the media, youth groups, labour unions and non-governmental organisations, as they have struggled to overcome yet another wave of marginalisation.

The final chapters address three key aspects of state policy: foreign policy, security and the economy. Gamal Hassan explains the remarkable stability of Egypt's foreign policy during a period of upheaval, and traces its fundamental drivers back to a consensus built during the Mubarak era. He contends that despite fears of a potential realignment, Egyptian foreign policy continues to fall back on positions that Mubarak established.

Hebatalla Taha examines Egypt's security challenges and argues that the state response is designed to bolster Sisi's strategy of consolidation, rather than provide holistic approaches to complex problems. She argues that continuous and escalating militarisation has exacerbated the insurgencies plaguing Egypt.

Finally, Mohamed El Dahshan analyses Egypt's difficult economic conditions. He notes that, despite a popular desire for reform, every government since 2011 has avoided hard decisions, and bowed to political expediency rather than pursuing a strategic vision. Although the Sisi-led government's apparent economic dynamism appears to have been well received, El Dahshan finds that government policies remain flawed and unlikely to reverse the effects of five years of stagnation.

Notes

[1] Marc Lynch, 'Calvinball in Cairo'. http://foreignpolicy.com/2012/06/18/calvinball-in-cairo.

CHAPTER ONE

The transition: from Mubarak's fall to the 2014 presidential election

Professor Nathan J. Brown

The forced departure of Egypt's long-time president, Hosni Mubarak, on 11 February 2011 was widely hailed as a popular revolution, not only in Egypt, but worldwide. And in many respects it was: a cascading series of demonstrations suddenly rendered the country ungovernable by a president whose tenure had extended almost three decades and who appeared to be slowly arranging his own succession. But the legal form his deposition took was a 'constitutional declaration' by the country's Supreme Council of the Armed Forces (SCAF) – a body nominally headed by the president himself but in effect operating independently – that Mubarak was no longer president and that the SCAF would oversee a transition to a new political system. That announcement, which all political forces that had supported the uprising welcomed and all state institutions accepted, contained many underappreciated contradictions. A democratic transition was supposed to be combined with unchecked military rule; a popular uprising decided happily to leave the state apparatus intact; a non-ideological movement simply chose at first to ignore the deep divisions within its own ranks.

The 40 months between Mubarak's departure and the inauguration of President Abdel Fattah Al-Sisi saw all these contradictions explode with full force. In the end, certain mechanical aspects of democracy did indeed emerge, and the memory of the uprising retained some political force and some established patterns that subsequent protest movements could draw on. But the tensions that were overlooked in February 2011 were resolved, at least for the moment, by the reassertion of a strong presidency and an unaccountable and authoritarian state apparatus – the very targets of the uprising.[1]

The revolution and its contradictions

Egypt's 2011 uprising was about many things, but among the chief forces animating it was a feeling that had grown surprisingly widespread, even to the point of becoming axiomatic among large swathes of Egyptian society: a small minority, who were accountable to no one, monopolised authority and used it for their own benefit. A consensus quickly formed in public squares throughout the country that it was necessary to reconstruct the political order, and perhaps transform the nature of prevailing social and economic relations, to solve Egypt's enormous problems and ensure that the country's assets were deployed to serve popular needs.

The variety of forces that could subscribe to such a view grew extremely wide. Labour protests had been mounting for years and contributed to the sense, accurate or not, that the rich were siphoning off Egypt's economic resources. Those at the top of the society seemed, in the eyes of many, to parlay political influence into wealth and sometimes even into immunity from the law with increasingly brazen ease. Many of those lower down in Egypt's vast array of institutions – whether ministries, educational institutions or public-sector companies – often felt that they were living in mini-autocracies, with power over their lives in the hands of despots who were either well connected or placed in their positions because of political allegiance. Citizens watched as the structures that promised them security instead terrorised their neighbourhoods. Viewers of state television or readers of state newspapers watched journalists trip over each other in unseemly sycophancy for the rulers. Pious individuals saw the elite as not merely selfish, but corrupting society's values. And young people looked on the system as having been designed to frustrate their ambitions.[2]

When hundreds of thousands of demonstrators – perhaps more – surprised themselves by uniting in Egypt's public squares in January and February 2011, they quickly came to feel that they spoke for the entire nation. And the forces of the state were quickly paralysed in the face of the popular uprising. They did not crumble, but neither could they respond coherently when the determination of the crowds became clear. After a few ineffectual attempts at negotiating an agreement, Mubarak found himself forced out by military officers he had appointed.

Momentarily the heroes of the crowd, the military assumed from the revolutionaries the mantle of speaking for the entire nation. But the apparent triumph of the various forces pressing for change had come so quickly that they had not had the opportunity to explore much common ground beyond their insistence that Mubarak leave, illustrated by the simplicity of the slogan *irhal* (leave). Among many unanswered questions was what sort of social and economic agenda any post-uprising regime would pursue; what kind of religious and cultural agenda would be appropriate; whether, how and how much various parts of the state apparatus should be reformed; and whether the revolutionary wave should extend more broadly to rooting out corrupt or stultifying practices in schools and workplaces throughout the country.

It was not that such questions were ignored but, swept up in the enthusiastic wave of national pride that followed the uprising, it seemed churlish to dwell on them. Only the despised *feloul* (remnants) of the old regime questioned the basic path the country was on. In March 2011, when asked if the judiciary was divided, a senior judge who was associated with the faction of the judiciary that eschewed confrontation with the Mubarak presidency told me: 'Everyone is with the revolution now!' Also a matter of startlingly little debate was how the revolution had been completely entrusted to a senior military leadership.

Egypt's first transition

The SCAF's transition plan was assembled partly in secret and partly by an ad hoc committee of jurists that developed what it first described as a set of amendments to the suspended 1971 constitution. Those amendments would be submitted to a popular referendum. The plan only made the confusion that followed Mubarak's downfall worse. Why revive a document for which few had any affection? Why begin elections with such a limited referendum? Why elect new officials – a president and a parliament – under the old framework rather than drafting a comprehensive new one?

As the process moved forward, two aspects became immediately clear. Firstly, the SCAF itself was monopolising all decisions over the process. Indeed, days before the referendum on constitutional amendments the SCAF revealed that it would issue a new constitutional declaration no matter what the result of the referendum. A few days after the referendum the SCAF issued an entirely new document (including the articles voters had approved) rather than reviving the suspended 1971 constitution. That governing document was neither explained nor justified; it was simply imposed by fiat.

Secondly, the choices that the SCAF was making had significant political implications; Egyptians quickly discovered that
there was no such thing as an impartial process. That quickly
led to suspicions of hidden agendas and secret deals; indeed,
all political actors seemed convinced that their rivals were
trying to get the SCAF on their side. Islamists in general, and
the Muslim Brotherhood in particular, quickly concluded that
the sooner – and more often – Egyptians voted, the more their
stock would be likely to rise. While they did not expect a majority – and indeed initially suggested they did not even want one
– Brotherhood leaders realised that they had more electoral
experience and organisation than their rivals, and the quick
succession of a constitutional referendum, and parliamentary
then presidential elections meant the Islamists could become
the leading coherent voice in the cacophonous political scene.
Non-Islamists came to the same calculation. Realising too late
that the SCAF's plan was stacked against them, they sought to
modify it by launching a 'constitution first' campaign, suggesting that a presidential council should govern Egypt while
the slow process of writing the constitution played out. The
proposal made a certain sense because it sought to establish
the rules of the game before the game began. But it was also
easily seen precisely for what it was: an attempt to outflank
the Islamists and to cut the popular voice out of the process in
favour of an elite deal.

The post-uprising jockeying therefore led to two developments that were ultimately fatal to many of the hopes of
revolutionary leaders. Firstly, it split the various civilian camps
in ways they did not fully understand and were unprepared to
cope with. Having lived under authoritarianism, members of
the suddenly victorious revolutionary coalition had directed
most of their anger and attention at the old regime, and they
were not used to dealing with each other. To be sure, Islamists,

leftists, nationalists and liberals had tried to build cross-ideological coalitions in the decade or so prior to Mubarak's overthrow, and had made tentative but sincere attempts to explore each other's priorities and find common ground. But those efforts were anaemic and shallow in comparison to those in other countries where prolonged struggle had led the opposition to develop more detailed joint platforms and plans. By summer 2011, it was already clear that all political tendencies had developed expertise primarily in talking amongst themselves. And much of that talk was about the nefarious intentions, hidden agendas and bad faith of their rivals. Competition and pluralism are necessary to democracy, but in Egypt these things were developing without any ground rules, mutual acceptance or experience of coping with such divisions.

The second underappreciated development was how the state apparatus had survived the uprising and managed to fend off intense pressures for change. In spring 2011, influential parts of Egyptian society seemed to be experiencing a moment comparable to 1968 in the West: hopes and fears about fundamental change abounded as did a sense that the youth were an irrepressible but unpredictable force, and that all established ways of doing things were now open to question. Inside Egyptian institutions, pressure very often came from below: an insistence that old leaders step aside or be held accountable for alleged misdeeds; the use of revolutionary slogans and demands to enact locally what had just been accomplished nationally. Very few of those feelings, overwhelming as they were, proved accurate. Instead, most Egyptian institutions survived intact. Changes were occasionally made at the top, and security forces and police apparatus kept a low profile for a little while. But the unanimity of support for the revolution made it possible for anyone to claim its mantle, and all but a few could deflect the pressures against them.

The process the SCAF had outlined in March 2011 continued,[3] but it certainly did not micromanage all the details. The SCAF was content to defer to negotiation among civilian political forces on important issues, such as drawing up electoral law for the parliamentary elections slated for late 2011. More ominously for the military, however, was that while it held all the cards in the short term, in the longer term it had designed a process that might empower civilian actors. And in the meantime, it was increasingly held to account for governing Egypt – sometimes badly. It was depleting its political capital by becoming implicated in attempts to end protests, as well as failing to address the continued deterioration of public services.

The election results came as a shock for most political forces: the Muslim Brotherhood was just shy of a parliamentary majority, and a new Salafi party, al-Nour, burst onto the scene, with over one-fifth of the seats. The parliament had very few powers under the SCAF's interim rules, but it was responsible for designating those who would write the permanent constitution. Non-Islamists were confused and outraged. Some attempted to maintain the revolutionary momentum, but the centre of attention was clearly shifting from the streets to the electoral arena, parliament and the Constituent Assembly. And they had little means of exerting influence in those arenas other than to abstain in protest. A deal on a consensual constitutional assembly fell through, and the Islamists in parliament used their majority to give themselves a leading voice in the process. Their opponents decided to sit much of the process out.

As the presidential election approached, state institutions also showed signs of panic. An administrative court disbanded the first Constituent Assembly on the grounds that it was not representative – even though it had been chosen by elected representatives. The Supreme Constitutional Court dissolved the lower house of the parliament, Magles al-Shaab, because it found the electoral law had violated past rulings about the rights of independents to contest seats. And the SCAF for its part issued a new supplementary constitutional declaration that reserved considerable authority for itself even after the election of a president.

The election of Muhammad Morsi, who had been in prison when the uprising broke out and was now moving into the presidential palace, was a further shock to the system.[4] His move to the palace was treated with triumphalism among his supporters, and with deep suspicion by Non-Islamists and a state apparatus that had, if anything, been arrayed against the Brotherhood for many years and was suddenly, nominally, subservient to one of its leaders.

The Morsi presidency

Morsi thus entered the presidency with a difficult choice before him. He was Egypt's first president to come from outside the state apparatus, and many civilian political forces had very reluctantly lent him their support towards the end of the campaign, giving him a narrow victory over his opponent, Ahmad Shafiq, a retired general and Mubarak's last prime minister. But if Morsi tried to craft a coalition out of these forces, he was hardly assured of success – they remained deeply suspicious of him and seemed to have trouble accepting their electoral defeat – and might only further alienate the state apparatus. He could, alternatively, try to come to terms with the state apparatus, in preparation for governing. His initial steps, in which he saluted even the abusive Egyptian police, suggested that he might try to straddle both paths at the same time. However, his early steps away from a civil coalition and towards mollifying the state proved definitive, and forced him further down the path of attempting to placate the state rather than reform it. The strategy, if it was that, was awkwardly pursued and proved untenable after only a year in office.

Yet Morsi's initial efforts seemed a bit more artful. He tried and failed to bring the parliament back, stymied by the courts. He then turned to the military and managed to negotiate with the SCAF to retire some of its senior officers and transfer its residual political powers back to the presidency. The Constituent Assembly continued its work, even as Non-Islamists continued to protest against the body. Morsi appointed commissions of inquiry to examine the violence that security bodies had inflicted on civilians since 2011 and attempted to appoint a cabinet with some non-Islamist political forces. The appeal to Non-Islamists failed to persuade many, however. Part of the problem was the uncompromising stance the opposition had taken and its general failure to develop any realistic demands that reflected electoral outcomes. But a large part of the responsibility lay with Morsi and the Brotherhood: they offered little, sometimes showed contempt for the developing civilian opposition and offered at best very junior roles to those who accepted their leadership. They managed to attract some technocrats and non-partisan figures, but the presidency's political base was dangerously narrow.

At first, relations with the state apparatus appeared to be improving. The military seemed to accept Morsi as president, as he completely shelved the matter of security-sector reform. He appointed an old-school interior minister whom the security forces had chosen from their own ranks. Morsi ignored the commissions of inquiry that he himself had formed. Some new officials were appointed (Islamists or their sympathisers were given a few provincial governorships and a few other top positions), leading the Brotherhood's opponents to decry the 'Brotherhoodisation of the state', but in fact the extent of personnel changes was not that large. The movement largely seemed to wish to placate the most powerful parts of the state (the military and security forces) and ignore or bypass others (such as the foreign ministry). Morsi picked a series of battles with the judiciary, however, seeing it as arrayed against his presidency, a perception that was half true and half self-fulfilling prophecy.

Up until November 2012, the Morsi presidency seemed to be slowly succeeding. But that month, confrontation between the president and his opponents led to a crisis from which Egypt never recovered. Apparently convinced that his civilian opponents were conspiring with elements of the judiciary and perhaps others within the state to disband the Constituent Assembly and even precipitate a series of events that would restore the military's political role, Morsi issued his own constitutional declaration moving the constitutional process outside of court review and dismissing the public prosecutor, substituting his own pick for the job. The Constituent Assembly rushed out a draft in an unseemly all-night session.

These moves galvanised the opposition into re-launching street protests; a series of attacks on Brotherhood offices led the movement to conclude that it was under a physical attack from which the police would not protect it. The Brotherhood called out its own supporters to defend the presidential palace, and they did so with violence. There was now not only bitterness between Morsi and his opponents but also blood. But by the end of the year, Morsi and his supporters could congratulate themselves on having won. Their constitution was approved by popular referendum and the opposition seemed to be dissolving into feuding and ineffectual groups of intellectuals and politicians without an organised constituency.

But success proved illusory. The security forces used their autonomy to work as they saw fit, and showed little evidence of their loyalty to the president. Indeed, they seemed to be leaking information, whether accurate or not, that portrayed the Brotherhood in a bad light, politically and legally. The state apparatus was actively working to undermine the president, who was nominally its head. The head of the religious establishment, Ali Gomaa, progressively distanced himself from the Brotherhood; the military rejected the idea of civilian control, and key members of the judiciary made it clear that they regarded Morsi's rule as illegitimate – an enmity he and his supporters returned with gusto. Indeed, in the government's final months, the upper house of parliament, Magles al-Shura, was drafting legislation to justify a purge of senior members of the judiciary.

Morsi had neither the skills nor the inclination to build a broader support base outside the state. The deepening gap among civilian political forces prompted attempts at mediation, but they fell through because of the top-heavy nature of the opposition (it was not clear who the self-proclaimed leaders of the opposition represented), their fractious nature and difficulty in articulating clear and consensual demands – but also because the Brotherhood made a clear calculation that the groups were not worth the effort it would take to bring them on board. The underappreciated problem for the Morsi presidency was that it was in charge of a state apparatus it could not control, yet it was still saddled with public responsibility of governance. Aggravating its low level of control was the awkward reality that even after the approval of the constitution, Egypt was still in transition and the basic political framework of the country was incomplete. The lower house of parliament had not been recalled and the Islamist-dominated upper house could not pass a draft that the country's constitutional court had approved, as the Brotherhood's own constitution now required.

The combination proved politically explosive. In spring 2013, a new youth-led opposition movement, Tamarod (Rebel), suddenly gained traction with a petition calling for a new presidential election. Reports of collusion among Tamarod's leaders with security services seem credible. But there was also no doubt that the campaign gave voice to a popular mood, at least in some parts of the country, that the Morsi presidency was a failure, and that it was too long to wait until the next presidential election in 2016. The movement called for mass protests on 30 June, and the Brotherhood responded by calling out its own supporters in a series of counter-demonstrations. As confrontation brewed, the military stepped in and threatened that it would have to take (unspecified) action. Given that opposition leaders openly hoped for military intervention, this hardly discouraged them. When the protests were indeed massively attended, the two sides prepared themselves for confrontation. The military dropped any pretence of neutrality, and on 3 July its leader, Sisi, announced that Morsi had been removed from office.

Not only had the opposition successfully provoked a military coup, but the new regime arrested senior Brotherhood leaders and held many incommunicado. Flanked by senior officials and with the support of most civilian political forces, Sisi appointed the chief justice of the constitutional court, Adly Mansour, as acting president and announced a 'road map', which Mansour later elaborated on, to amend the constitution and move towards new parliamentary and presidential elections. Proclaiming itself a second revolution – or the completion of the 2011 revolution against Mubarak – the movement to overthrow Morsi promised full democracy. It did not deliver on its promise, except in the most formal sense.

After 3 July: the state reassembled

The road map of July 2013 described a clear sequence of events: the constitution would be amended, parliamentary elections would be held and then a presidential election would complete the transition. It also promised a more ethical media, attempts at national reconciliation and better integration of young people into decision-making. It did not really meet any of these goals. Rather than amending the constitution, the entire document was systematically rewritten; the presidential election was held first; and the broader goals related to the press, reconciliation, and youth were simply forgotten about.[5]

Part of the problem was that the political situation deteriorated so quickly, because the Brotherhood refused to accept Morsi's ouster as final or legitimate, and the new regime responded to Brotherhood protests with ferocity. For weeks after the coup, Morsi's supporters came out to demonstrate, and Brotherhood leaders who had evaded arrest gave increasingly fiery speeches. A procession of international mediators was occasionally allowed to speak to imprisoned Brotherhood leaders, but neither side seemed interested in reaching an accommodation.

Occasional violence broke out, with security forces some-times appearing anxious to use deadly force to drive home the message that organised demonstrations – particularly near sensitive locations – were unacceptable. On 15 August they finally moved against the main Brotherhood encamp-ments, with unprecedented force and killing hundreds of protesters. Morsi supporters responded by attacking police stations and churches around the country. The Brotherhood itself continued to disavow violence, but it was clear that some of its supporters considered hurling Molotov cocktails at police exempt from the ban. Moreover, the heated atmo-sphere in Cairo and other cities provided an opening for radical Islamist groups to move directly against state targets in a more concerted and unambiguously violent way. The groups, initially based among Egypt's marginalised popula-tion in the Sinai peninsula, stepped up their activities in the aftermath of the coup.

A second factor aggravating the political situation was rhetorical escalation on all sides, as public and private media turned against Morsi and the Brotherhood with stunning vitriol. Routinely referred to as 'terrorists' or blamed for shooting themselves in the violent demonstrations, Brotherhood members found themselves the target of enormous official and unofficial hatred. The degree of dehumanisation resembled what might be expected in the midst of a bloody civil war.

The formal process of political reconstruction continued in this unpromising atmosphere. State institutions that had weathered the storm of 2011 suddenly found themselves redeemed. Official media, reviled for their sycophancy towards Mubarak, found that their adulation of the new order struck a chord with many Egyptians. The religious establishment, part of the state structure, moved to assert its control over mosques and preachers. The police found that when they suppressed Brotherhood protesters, they were treated by many as heroes. Parts of the judiciary joined in the campaign to hold Brotherhood members responsible for the violence, and meted out harsh sentences with enthusiasm. And the military, which was blamed by many for mismanaging affairs in 2011 and 2012, found itself summoned back to politics, with Sisi lionised by private and public media alike. It was difficult to tell how deeply the mood of retribution against the Brotherhood and worship of Sisi went, but many among the political elite and middle and upper classes of major cities were swept along with it.

Mansour appointed a committee to redraft the 2012 constitution. State bodies were heavily represented in the committee, and most seemed to get what they wanted in the document. The military was in effect insulated from civilian oversight, and the police received a degree of protection as well. Judges got guarantees of independence, and the leadership of the religious establishment received its own assurances. The document, approved by referendum in January 2014, attempted to close loopholes inserted in previous documents to rob constitutional guarantees of most of their meaning. But this occurred in an atmosphere in which security forces made clear that they would either ignore the guarantees – some of those campaigning against the referendum, for example, were put on trial, suggesting that the document's guarantees might even be stillborn – or find ways around them – by concocting charges against political opponents – or simply fill in very general constitutional and legal language with authoritarian practices, such as when a new protest law was issued and immediately used to levy extremely harsh sentences against those who protested without a permit. The new regime seemed uncomfortable with the very kind of mass mobilisation that had brought it into being.

Sisi himself stood aloof from public involvement for most of the process, but his somewhat evasive answers about whether or not he would seek the presidency were enough to discourage any serious competition from arising. He finally negotiated with his military colleagues to receive their backing, rearranged the high command to leave behind what promised to be a loyal structure, and then plunged into the presidential race. It was not much of a campaign. Sisi barely appeared in person; although he gave a few in-depth media interviews, they tended to combine vague invocations of patriotism with either unrealistic visions (a string of international airports and satellites cities to be built by a nearly bankrupt state) or strangely detailed ones (persuading Egyptians to use energy-efficient light bulbs). What was missing was any policy vision or ideology beyond duty, God and country.

Conclusion: the Sisi presidency

Swept into office in an election in which his spoiled ballots outpolled his sole opponent, Sisi nonetheless faces a daunting agenda. He has continued to operate under something of an international cloud, at least in his relations with Western governments. Although Sisi has been accepted as president, and even welcomed in a few Western capitals, the widespread repression, apparent mishandling of the incipient radical Islamist insurgency and lack of an economic vision have set off deep misgivings among many potential partners. The spirit of protest of 2011 and 2013 may have diminished somewhat, but given that the population has twice risen against its president, and smaller-scale protests and strikes have become routine, Sisi may not have unlimited time. The hollowing out of formal politics – the predictable presidential race, the likelihood of a divided parliament and a weak party system – may continue to steer popular political energies in ways that any regime would find difficult to manage.

Morsi was given one year before he was ousted; Sisi, with the state apparatus solidly behind him, has already had longer. But that state itself may prove to be a problem for him. Its various parts shook off the hand of the Mubarak presidency; it is not clear they will answer to Sisi. Nor is it clear where he would lead them if he could. Egypt's problems in almost every realm are enormous; Sisi has given every sign of understanding their extent, but few of his ideas for solutions.

Notes

[1] I have examined this trajectory from the perspective of democratic mechanisms in Nathan J. Brown, 'Egypt's Failed Transition', *Journal of Democracy*, vol. 24, no. 3, October 2013, pp. 45–58.

[2] See Mona el-Ghobashy, 'The Praxis of the Egyptian Revolution', *Middle East Report*, vol. 41, no. 258, Spring 2011.

[3] International Crisis Group, 'Lost in Transition: The World According to Egypt's SCAF', Middle East/North Africa Report, no. 12124, April 2012, available at http://www.crisisgroup.org/~/media/Files/Middle%20East%20North%20Africa/North%20Africa/Egypt/121-lost-in-transition-the-world-according-to-egypts-scaf.pdf.

[4] For an original and sophisticated analysis of Egyptian voting patterns, see Tarek Masoud, *Counting Islam: Religion, Class, and Elections in Egypt* (Cambridge: Cambridge University Press, 2014).

[5] See Nathan J. Brown, 'Grading Egypt's Road Map to Democracy', *Foreign Policy*, 5 May 2014, http://foreignpolicy.com/2014/05/05/grading-egypts-roadmap-toward-democracy.

CHAPTER TWO

Courts and police in revolution

Professor Ellis Goldberg

Hosni Mubarak resigned as president on 11 February 2011 in the wake of unexpected and massive demonstrations, strikes and attacks on institutions of public order. The police vanished from the streets and in some places units of the armed forces replaced them; the legislature, under attack following what was widely seen as a fraudulent election several months earlier, was paralysed.[1] Surprisingly, the judiciary, some of whose members had fought a widely publicised battle for independence five years earlier, emerged as an important political force.[2] The armed forces, presumed guarantors of the regime, stepped in to ensure that Mubarak left office. Twice in three years, with significant popular support each time, the military proved to be the ultimate centre of power in the country. And Egypt's immense administrative bureaucracy continued to function, albeit at a slower and more cautious pace than before.

The lively, contentious and unresolved academic debate about the state, revolution and mass uprisings across centuries and continents will not detain us here. From it we will simply extract two basic ideas. Firstly, the modern state is defined by its institutions: a large bureaucracy through which the executive administers society according to existing legislation; a legislative body responsible for making laws, but neither for implementing regulations nor enforcing procedures; and a court system divided into jurisdictions of fact-finding and review.[3] Secondly, the effectiveness of the state in governing the territory it claims to control rests on a division of labour in the administration of force. The police maintain domestic order, while the army maintains the sovereignty of the state. Almost invariably – and Egypt is no exception – the armed forces train for combat with heavy weaponry, whereas the police train to suppress local and small-scale violations of the law.

Egypt's judiciary and armed forces have especially strong corporate identities and powerful interests in maintaining their institutional structures. Egyptian political scientist Ashraf al-Sherif describes contemporary Egypt as a 'state of fiefdoms' (*taifas* state), in which the various institutions of the state are independent because they have separate patterns of recruitment, training and promotion.[4] They accomplish these goals by co-optation and by what amounts to self-selection within a group with common educational, social and political preferences. Thus the children of judges, army and police officers themselves become judges, army and police officers. Promotion is governed largely by seniority and connections. Relatively little lateral movement occurs in this system, and a variety of ideal and material interests enable members to protect the independence of their body from external influence. For example, several institutional mechanisms strengthen the cohesion of the judiciary as a corps, allowing judges to reach some level of internal coherence on issues as distinct as professional organisation, compensation and substantive discussion of law. A specific example is the Judges Club, founded in 1939, which provides judges with access to goods and services, as well as a venue in which discussions about law and the judicial branch can be held.

After Mubarak left office, the armed forces and the judiciary were the institutions most Egyptians looked to for stability and a resolution of what many perceived as a revolutionary crisis of governance. A variety of politically charged questions that were properly the purview of either an executive or legislative branch were deferred to the judiciary. These ranged from issues on the basic structure of political institutions and organisations to symbolically important but marginal concerns. Thus, the courts rather than the Supreme Council of the Armed Forces (SCAF) dissolved the former ruling National Democratic Party (NDP)[5] and locally elected bodies.[6] It was also the courts that stripped Mubarak's name from public buildings, squares and even a Cairo subway station.

The police

Activists from many organisations called for demonstrations on Police Day, 25 January 2011. Thousands of protesters marched to Tahrir Square in downtown Cairo, where the police violently dispersed them with clubs and tear gas. Wider protests broke out, especially in cities around the Delta, and organisers called for mass protests on 28 January, known as the 'Day of Rage'. That evening, the police lines either broke down or were withdrawn by then-interior minister Habib al-Adly. Demonstrators then surged into Tahrir Square, and the armed forces entered the streets and squares of the capital and other towns. The mass protests, strikes and demonstrations were generally peaceful. However, more than 100 police stations and several prisons were destroyed, accompanied by the murder of a police general and the freeing of thousands of prison inmates. Within hours, the police ceased to exist as a coherent body and no organised police – whether traffic police, ordinary police officers or the semi-militarised state security forces – were on the streets. In many neighbourhoods, local committees took on the task of providing security.[7]

The Egyptian police force is a centralised bureaucracy under the control of the interior ministry.[8] At least since 1923, Egyptian constitutional experts have understood the police to have all necessary powers to ensure public order, unless otherwise specified.[9] As early as the 1970s, president Anwar Sadat began to rely on the State Security Agency as a counterweight to the armed forces, and the interior ministry, including its intelligence services, began to displace the army.[10] The increased role of the ministry did not translate into higher salaries or educational attainment and thus corruption in the police grew.[11] Between 1970 and 2011, when Egypt was nearly continuously under a state of emergency, the interior ministry expanded from 214,000 to 1.5 million.[12] As it expanded, the quality of the legal education of its officers declined. Their experience was increasingly that the superiors condoned violence, and very few Coptic Christians, graduates of al-Azhar University or former members of the Muslim Brotherhood were admitted.[13] The widespread perception that no clear line separated the police from criminals was popularised in the 2001 film *A Citizen, a Detective, and a Thief*.

The police force comprises many different kinds of officers, from unarmed police in uniform who direct traffic to fearsomely armoured units of the Central Security Forces. Anger towards the police played an important role in sparking off the uprising and, although police reform was an important issue, it was never seriously undertaken.[14] A period of several months, known as the 'security collapse', followed the uprising. During this time, public order was maintained by the armed forces and unexpectedly high levels of social cohesion, resulting in popular committees – groups of civilians who decided to take security into their own hands.[15]

Ending police brutality was a major theme of the uprising and the image of a disfigured Khaled Said, beaten to death in summer 2010 in Alexandria, was an important driver of public anger. Reform of Egyptian policing would have required transforming the interior ministry, including its training and hiring policies, as well as the legal system of emergency law under which it operated. Interim prime minister Essam Sharaf appointed Mansour el-Essawy as interior minister on 5 March 2011. Essawy renamed the State Security Investigation Services the Homeland Security Services and claimed it would no longer employ abusive practices. Despite the forcible retirement of hundreds of officers, almost no real change in the ministry took place.[16]

President Muhammad Morsi proposed significant reform of the police in the first 100 days of his administration, including amending the Police Act, restructuring the security agencies and the interior ministry, and reviewing police training. Although the new government increased police benefits, it made no other changes in the security structure.[17] Despite being appointed under Morsi, interior minister Mohamed Ibrahim played a key role in the deadly assault on two pro-Morsi protests in Cairo on 14 August 2013, during which more than 800 people were killed. Ibrahim participated in the revival of the Mubarak-era police state under acting president Adly Mansour and later President Abdel Fattah Al-Sisi.[18]

The courts

In his resignation, announced by vice-president Omar Suleiman on 11 February 2011, Mubarak entrusted the management of the country's affairs to the SCAF. This was taken to mean that, for an unspecified period of time, the SCAF would hold legislative and executive power. The judiciary remained intact and in place. It was not surprising that trial judges remained in place if their role in the system was analogous to that of the officials in the administrative bureaucracy. More remarkable was that the highest levels of the court system, including the Supreme Constitutional Court (SCC), the appellate system and the administrative courts remained intact, active and entrusted with the legitimacy to make consequential decisions.[19] Unlike any other similar upheaval in the previous two centuries, the Egyptian revolution was one in which legality and the interpretive decisions of the country's highest judges played a dominant role in its outcome. Later, an attempt by a freely elected president to affect the courts prompted the opposition that ultimately led to his ousting by the military. The often-derided military hierarchy was, at the moment of crisis, the sole institution willing and able to assume absolute power.

The standing of the judiciary in Egypt during the republican regime fluctuated: legal education had become widespread and somewhat devalued early in this period, but judicial careers were still eagerly sought after.[20] After significant areas of the economy were returned to private ownership and foreign investors arrived, some lawyers once again found the calling lucrative. Gamal Abdel Nasser, Sadat and Mubarak all used tactics to co-opt and subordinate the judiciary and to prevent it from interfering with the state's economic and repressive policies. Between 1990 and 2010 this primarily meant facilitating privatisation in the economy and allowing the state to carve out an area of exceptional justice, through military and security courts, with which to pursue an armed Islamist opposition and the mass movement of the Brotherhood. The judiciary was more than willing to support privatisation, but institutionally many members – especially in the higher courts – had significant reservations about repression. The wholesale attack on individual rights presented problems for some liberal judges, and the attempt to create an entire secondary court apparatus was troubling for others.

Among many reasons for the importance of the judiciary immediately after the uprising, a broad consensus held that Egyptians wanted something like the rule of law to prevail over emerging lawlessness in society and the arbitrary authority of the state, which had been criticised internationally as the rule of impunity.[21] None of the prominent political forces – from the Brotherhood to Salafi movements or the liberal left – sought to establish exceptional courts. Despite the creation of popular committees to protect order in many places in the first months of 2011, no call followed to arm such committees or organise them in a coherent structure. The SCAF replaced the old constitution with an interim document, allotting itself not only executive and legislative powers, but also the power to act as a Constituent Assembly as well, while leaving the structure of the judiciary – including the SCC – intact. The interim constitution also made the Appellate Court rather than the legislature the judge in disputes over seating legislators in the wake of contested elections.

Many observers saw 2011 as the prelude to a democratic transition.[22] This implied that the state institutions, apart from the executive and legislative authorities, were sufficiently sound to retain within the structure of a new government. That the major tasks of the transitional period were to write a new constitution and elect a new legislative and executive fitted in with this perspective. The SCAF promised that it would hold legislative and presidential elections under its constitutional declaration, and it did. It rapidly became clear that the courts would continue to play a role in adjudicating the kinds of disputes they had addressed during the Mubarak era. In elections from 1986 onwards, the SCC had created its own jurisprudence about which electoral rules violated the constitution, and its members felt empowered to pursue these rules even after the upheaval of 2011.

The constitution and elections

The first election made clear that religion could be a powerful mobilising tool. What was less clear was how many voters had mobilised to support the Brotherhood or Salafi currents, and how many saw themselves as supporting both Islam and the armed forces. The first election, a referendum on a set of six amendments to the old constitution, was held in March 2011. Several prominent jurists drafted the amendments, at the insistence of the armed forces, and the referendum became one basis for the SCAF's claim to represent the popular will. Working in tandem with the army, the Brotherhood and Salafi movements generated significant electoral support for the amendments by claiming that they preserved the Islamic character of the state that unnamed secularists and Christians hoped to remove. The referendum passed with 77% of the vote. Almost immediately, the SCAF broke the promise that the public was voting to amend the existing constitution. It issued a declaration that superseded the 1971 constitution but retained the amendments, which have remained in all subsequent constitutions.

In his capacity as the head of the SCAF with presidential powers, defence minister Muhammad Tantawi appointed a series of governments. His first prime minister, Essam Sharaf, replaced Mubarak's final appointment, Ahmad Shafiq, who left after little more than a month in office. Sharaf acquired popular respect in 2006 when he resigned as transport minister after a dispute with the government. He gained further support when he addressed a rally in Tahrir Square next to Brotherhood leader Mohammed al-Beltagy and asserted that his legitimacy lay in popular mobilisation. Despite his appearance with Beltagy, Sharaf's own ministers were drawn from the ranks of liberal, leftist and old-line Nasserist politicians. Sharaf's tenure was punctuated by persistent conflicts that he was largely unable to manage, often because he lacked the necessary political power.

Besides an uprising in Qena, he had to deal with several incidents of severe violence against Christians, including a pitched battle that resulted in the burning of a church in Greater Cairo and the deaths of nearly 25 protesters – mostly Christians – in downtown Cairo on 9 October 2011 when they were run over by armoured personnel carriers manned by members of the armed forces.[23]

The final weeks of Sharaf's term as prime minister were overwhelmed by conflicts over the forthcoming constitution. In early November 2011 one of Sharaf's deputy prime ministers, Ali al-Selmi, published a proposal that the forthcoming constitution be written by representatives of Egypt's already existing institutions, that the SCAF retain a veto over the constitution and that the military budget be constitutionally protected from civilian oversight. The plan contradicted the SCAF's earlier constitutional declaration, which stated that the new Constituent Assembly would be chosen unconditionally by a freely elected legislature. It also prompted a series of demonstrations in Tahrir Square, which led to street fighting in several neighbouring streets and resulted in the deaths of 25 people. Toward the end of November public attention as well as that of activists turned toward the legislative elections, and the Selmi plan was shelved.

The SCAF had agreed to transfer power to a newly elected legislature.[24] As had been the case in Egypt since 1923, it was to be a bicameral body, with primary authority invested in the more broadly based lower house (Magles al-Shaab – People's Assembly). The upper house (Magles al-Shura – Consultative Council) had less power: the president appointed one-third of its members, providing the executive with a measure of indirect control over the legislative branch.

The parliamentary elections were exceptionally contentious, not least because of the blatant fraud that had marked the 2010 contests, in which the ruling NDP won 420 of 444 open seats. After months of conflict, the SCAF agreed that the election would be held in three rounds under a mixed system of proportional representation; two-thirds of seats would be elected as individual candidacies and the rest under proportional representation. After months of debate and protest, it finally agreed to reverse the allocation of seats: two-thirds would be based on party lists and one-third individual candidacies. The SCAF's initial proposal that only independents – that is, non-party members – run for the individual seats was discarded.

Earlier court decisions had mandated that members of the judiciary, broadly defined, should oversee legislative and presidential elections. To accomplish this, the parliamentary elections were held in two sets of three rounds: elections to the lower house ran from the end of November 2011 to early January 2012, and to the upper house from late January to February 2012. The Brotherhood won about 47% of the seats of the lower house, and Salafi parties won about 25%. Turnout dropped sharply for the upper house; the Islamists won a larger victory and would therefore dominate the new legislature. Unfortunately, even after the revolution the legislature counted for relatively little because the president still appointed the cabinet (the Council of Ministers). The stage was set for an even more crucial electoral conflict that occupied the country's attention until June: the presidential election. Egypt was, and largely remains, a strong presidential system in which the executive has extensive constitutional and statutory power.

The 2012 presidential election was the most open in Egypt's history and generated its own bitter legacy, as well as a brief period of hope. Despite an earlier assertion that the Brotherhood did not plan to field a candidate, it nominated businessman Khairat al-Shater, one of the most prominent leaders of the movement. The decision for Shater to run was controversial, not only because the Brotherhood had promised not to field a candidate, but also because it had already expelled another leader, Abdel Moneim Aboul Fotouh, when he announced his own candidacy. A third candidate, Hazem Salah Abu Ismail, presented himself as a populist Salafi in opposition to Shater's more buttoned-down organisational presence and Aboul Fotouh's far greater openness to non-Islamist and liberal currents. Two candidates who had been affiliated to the Mubarak regime also joined the race: former general and prime minister Ahmad Shafiq, and former foreign minister Amr Moussa. Several more candidates represented other constituencies, notably the left.

The judiciary was quickly drawn into the presidential campaign when several candidates were accused of violating either constitutional or statutory requirements to run. The body overseeing the election, the Supreme Presidential Election Council (SPEC), was composed of judges from the country's highest courts. The SPEC determined that Shater and Abu Ismail were barred from running. The Brotherhood responded by replacing Shater with Morsi who was therefore perceived from the outset as a second-choice – and second-rate – candidate, earning him the pejorative nickname, 'the spare tyre' (el-stebn) by the opposition.

Egyptian presidential elections require the victor to gain more than 50% of the vote. With ten major candidates, two rounds were necessary. There were five leading candidates – Morsi, Shafiq, Aboul Fotouh, Moussa and left-wing populist Hamdeen Sabahi: Morsi and Shafiq each won about 25%, and the others trailed behind, with Moussa picking up 11%. The last round of voting was a run-off between Morsi and Shafiq. More than a year of revolutionary turmoil had left an electorate almost evenly divided between supporters of the old regime and supporters of the new.

The courts, as a body, were drawn deeper into politics as losing candidates in the parliamentary elections filed suits arguing that the elections had been unconstitutional because they allowed party members to run as members of lists and as individuals simultaneously. This accorded with the long-standing jurisprudence of the SCC and raised the possibility that the first openly and fairly elected legislature in Egyptian history would suffer the fate of several legislatures under Mubarak: dissolution by court order.

On 14 June, the Supreme Court affirmed a lower-court decision that the legislative elections had been unconstitutional, but it was up to the SCAF to determine the solution. The SCAF almost immediately dissolved the lower house, even though it had less extreme options open to it, such as declaring one-third of the seats vacant. Two weeks later, on 24 June, Morsi won the presidential run-off with 52% of the vote. He was inaugurated on 30 June, an event that immediately intensified his conflict with the courts and more specifically the SCC. The constitutional declaration called on Morsi to take the oath of office before the lower house or before the SCC if the house was dissolved. Responding to what he believed was a politically motivated decision by the SCC, Morsi initially refused to take the oath before the judges, and instead took a symbolic oath at a ceremony before a mass gathering in Tahrir Square.

Morsi as president

Having attained the presidency, the Brotherhood could form a government. Morsi and his advisers acknowledged that a Brotherhood government would be too narrowly based to be politically viable. The president may also have realised from the beginning that his majority in parliament was weak to begin with and getting weaker. In retrospect, it is also apparent that Morsi and the Brotherhood are likely to have profoundly misunderstood the official security structures they were dealing with. Given the social and organisational structures of the *taifas* state, significant change in the defence and interior (police) ministries would mean replacing many, if not most, of the officers, massive retraining of regular personnel, as well as completely redesigning the regulatory and statutory regimes. In August, following an attack by Islamist guerrillas on border guards in Sinai, Morsi replaced Tantawi and interior minister Mohamed Ibrahim, respectively, with Sisi and deputy interior minister Ahmad Gamal al-Din. Many initially viewed the replacement of Tantawi as proof that an elected civilian leadership finally controlled the armed forces.[25] At around the same time, Morsi appointed Ahmed Mekki, former deputy chief of the highest appellate court, as justice minister, and his brother Mahmoud Mekki, also a former appellate judge, as vice-president.

During its brief life the legislature had managed to choose the Constituent Assembly to write a new constitution. The majority of its members were from various Islamist parties, including the Brotherhood. After the high administrative court dissolved it, a second assembly was chosen, following extensive negotiations, but with the possibility that it too would be dissolved. It nevertheless began its work.

In late November, as renewed demonstrations around Tahrir Square turned violent, Morsi issued his own constitutional decree, which in effect dismissed the public prosecutor and shielded the Constituent Assembly, the Consultative Council and his own decrees from court oversight. This assertion of extra-constitutional authority and the attempt to diminish the authority of the judiciary provoked massive demonstrations, for and against Morsi. For a moment it appeared as if Tahrir Square would become the site where two distinctly different and opposing groups of more than 100,000 people each battled for supremacy. In the end Morsi's supporters decided not to march into the square, and confrontation was avoided. Morsi himself withdrew his constitutional declaration, but the Constituent Assembly rushed to complete the text of the constitution, because it feared that the courts would invalidate the assembly – itself the result of an unconstitutional legislature – and thereby the new constitution also.

By the end of 2012, the Brotherhood, which controlled the presidency, came into increasing conflict with other sectors of Egyptian society and members of the judiciary, over matters of principle, but also corporate interest.[26] Mahmoud Mekki resigned as vice-president in December 2012 and Ahmed Mekki as justice minister in April 2013, as Egyptian society and politics became highly polarised. This came to a head in June–July 2013, after a popular movement provided the armed forces, led by Sisi, with sufficient reason to stage a coup and remove Morsi. The army subsequently and violently dispersed pro-Morsi demonstrations, and nearly 1,000 people were killed.

Conclusion

This was not the first time that the military hierarchy had taken power. In 1952 a group of colonels overthrew the constitutional monarchy and parliament, as well as the general staff. It then re-made the armed forces and set Egypt on the road to a populist government, with a major role for state ownership. In 2013 the generals came to power in an informal coalition with the judiciary and the police.

Perhaps the most peculiar feature of the present regime is the degree to which the judiciary has retained an important institutional presence. Despite claims that the judiciary is subservient to the military, there is every reason to believe that the majority of the judges – for reasons of prestige, institutional solidarity and social preferment – are committed to the

Sisi government. On several occasions judges have gone out of their way to condemn former members of the Brotherhood to death, even when it was clear that the sentences were likely to be overturned or reduced on appeal. Jurists have also been aware that their power rests to a large degree on their assertions of independence, no matter how limited they may be.[27] The appointment of Ahmed el-Zend as justice minister in 2015 indicates the restoration of powerful figures from the Mubarak regime and the defeat of the current within the judiciary that supported the uprising. Zend served as president of the Judges Club from 2009 until his ministerial appointment. In 2012, while a judge on the Cairo Court of Appeals, he suggested that judges should refuse to supervise the presidential election that Morsi was expected to win.[28]

For now, Egypt has the appearance of a dictatorship, in which a nominally civilian government lightly shields the military from the direct gaze of the public. The judiciary may be a junior partner in this process, but will not be subservient.[29] The willingness of judges to impose death sentences and lengthy prison terms on members of the Brotherhood and other political opponents of the regime reflects their own beliefs. Concern that they be perceived as independent, and differences among judges, will also matter. Egyptian judges will therefore be far more likely than their colleagues in other dictatorships – from Chile to Russia to China – to release a few political prisoners who present no threat to the state, and to rule in favour of some of the thousands swept up in the assaults against the Brotherhood in 2013 and 2014. The Egyptian judiciary reflected and influenced the massive political conflicts the country experienced between 2011 and 2015. There is every reason to believe that this will continue to be the case.

Notes

1   Ali Farghali, the former chief judge of the Higher Administrative Courts, pointed out to a reporter that the 2010 People's Assembly could not meet the constitutional quorum required for its acts to be valid because more than half the seats had been declared void by judicial decisions. See 'Judges Call for Drafting New Constitution to Respect "Revolutionary Legitimacy"', al-Shorouq, 6 February 2011, p. 4.

2   The demand for a new constitution was not initially a demand of protesters or organisers of the 25 January or 28 January demonstrations. It first appeared in a declaration by 40 judges in solidarity with the protesters. See 'Egyptian Judges from Midan al-Tahrir: We Advise the President to Comply with the Nation's Demands Sparing Bloodshed and Protecting the Fatherland's Higher Interests', al-Masry al-Yawm, 31 January 2011, p. 3.

3   As with most accounts of the state, mine is based on one of Max Weber's formulations, specifically: 'In a modern state, the actual ruler is necessarily and unavoidably the bureaucracy'. See Guenther Roth and Claus Wittich (eds), Max Weber, Economy and Society (Berkeley, CA: University of California Press, 1978, Vol. 2), p. 1393. For one of many brief summations of contemporary views, see Christopher W. Morris, An Essay on the Modern State (Cambridge: Cambridge University Press, 1998), especially pp. 37–51.

4   Ashraf el-Sherif, 'Egypt's Post-Mubarak Predicament', Carnegie Endowment for International Peace, 29 January 2014, available at http://carnegieendowment.org/2014/01/29/egypt-s-post-mubarak-predicament.

5   Kristen Chick, 'Court Order to Dissolve Egypt's NDP Deals Body Blow to Old Power Structure', Christian Science Monitor, 17 April 2011, http://www.csmonitor.com/World/Middle-East/2011/0417/Court-order-to-dissolve-Egypt-s-NDP-deals-body-blow-to-old-power-structure.

6   The SCAF dissolved the People's Assembly in its communiqué no. 5 and suspended the constitution on 13 February 2011.

7   See 'Popular Squads Fill the Security Vacuum in the Streets', al-Masry al-Yawm, 31 January 2011, p. 1, and 'El-Adly Demands that the Police Return to Work', al-Masry al-Yawm, 31 January 2011, p. 1. In mid-February the armed forces were still providing police protection in many parts of Cairo; see 'The Armed Forces Strengthen Security Measures Around the Presidential Palace and Abu El-Gheit: The Army Has Intervened to Protect National Security from Adventurers', al-Masry al-Yawm, 11 February 2011, p. 4. An important retrospective by Yezid Sayegh describes the first weeks of the uprisings as a period when 'police cohesion and morale collapsed amid mass revulsion'. See Yezid Sayegh, 'Missed Opportunity: The Politics of Police Reform in Egypt and Tunisia', Carnegie Middle East Center Papers, 17 March 2015,

available at http://carnegie-mec.org/publications/?fa=59391.

8 On the origins of local policing as a dependency of centralised national government and specifically the council of ministers in 1876, see Abd al-Wahab Bakr, *Al-Bulis al-Misri 1922–1952* (Cairo: Maktabat Madbouli, 1987), p. 81.

9 White Ibrahim, *La Constitution Égyptienne du 19 Avril 1923* (Paris: Edouard Duchemin, 1924), p. 52.

10 Robert Springborg, *Mubarak's Egypt* (Boulder, CO: Westview Press, 1989), pp. 140–42.

11 *Ibid.*, p. 143.

12 Tawfik Aclimandos, 'Healing without Amputating? Security Sector Reform in Egypt', *Arab Reform Initiative*, September 2012, p. 2, available at http://www.arab-reform.net/sites/default/files/SSR_Egypt_T.Aclimandos_Sep12_Final_En.pdf.

13 *Ibid.*, p. 8.

14 Ibrahim al-Houdaiby, 'Changing Alliances and Continuous Oppression: The Rule of Egypt's Security Sector', *Arab Reform Initiative*, June 2014, available at http://www.arab-reform.net/sites/default/files/Houdaiby_-_Egypt_Security_Sector_-_June_2014.pdf.

15 See Mara Revkin and Yusuf Auf, 'Egypt's Fallen Police State Gives Way to Vigilante Justice', *Atlantic*, 3 April 2013, http://www.theatlantic.com/international/archive/2013/04/egypts-fallen-police-state-gives-way-to-vigilante-justice/274616/.

16 See Daniel Brumberg and Hesham Sallam, 'The Politics of Security Sector Reform in Egypt', *United States Institute of Peace Special Report 318*, October 2012, available at http://www.usip.org/sites/default/files/SR318_0.pdf. See also Matilda Johansson and Annelie Norton, 'Police Reform in Egypt – A Case Study', Umea Universitet, 2013, pp. 30–1, 38.

17 See Johansson and Norton, 'Police Reform in Egypt – A Case Study', pp. 38–40 and Sayegh, 'Missed Opportunity: The Politics of Police Reform in Egypt and Tunisia', p. 13. Sayegh argues, 'The Morsi administration abdicated management of the security sector entirely to the Ministry of the Interior'.

18 Sayegh, 'Missed Opportunity: The Politics of Police Reform in Egypt and Tunisia', pp. 14–15.

19 See Lama Abu-Odeh, 'Of Law and Revolution', *University of Pennsylvania Journal of International Law*, vol. 34, no. 2, 2013, pp. 341–63, especially p. 348.

20 Bruce K. Rutherford, *Egypt after Mubarak* (Princeton, NJ: Princeton University Press, 2008), p. 48.

21 For an acerbic view of how the rule of law looks from the point of view of judges and litigants alike, see Hussein Agrama, *Questioning Secularism* (Chicago, IL: University of Chicago Press, 2012), pp. 131–37.

22 US political scientists heralded the idea of democratic transition from the earliest days. See Alfred Stepan and Juan J. Linz, 'How Egypt Can make Democracy Work', *Atlantic*, 12 February 2011, http://www.theatlantic.com/international/archive/2011/02/how-egypt-can-make-democracy-work/71125/; and Nathan J. Brown, 'Egypt's Failed Transition', *Journal of Democracy*, vol. 24, no. 4, October 2013, pp. 45–58.

23 On fighting in Imbaba, see 'Violence, Discrimination and Political Unrest in Egypt', *Nisr al Nasr* blog, 23 May 2011, http://nisralnasr. blogspot.com/2011/05/violence-discrimination-and-political. html. On Maspero, see Anthony Shenoda, 'Public Christianity in a Revolutionary Egypt', Fieldsights–Hot Spots, Cultural Anthropology Online, 13 May 2013, http://www. culanth.org/fieldsights/234-public-christianity-in-a-revolutionary-egypt.

24 Hesham Sallam (ed.), *Egypt's Parliamentary Elections, 2011–2012* (Washington DC: Tadween Publishing, 2013).

25 Moataz El Fegiery, 'Crunch Time for Egypt's Civil–Military Relations', FRIDE Policy Brief no. 134, August 2012, http://fride.org/descarga/pb_134_crunch_time_for_egypts_civil_military_relations.pdf; Bruce Maddy-Weitzman, 'From Sinai to Cairo: Morsy Makes his Move', *Mideast Monitor, Jerusalem Report*, Moshe Dayan Center, 10 September 2012; Steven A. Cook, 'Brother Knows Best: How Egypt's New President is Outsmarting the Generals', in *Morsi's Egypt*, POMEPS Briefing no. 13, 20 August 2012. For a dissenting view, see Ellis Goldberg, 'The Morsi "coup": Coup d'état, coup de grâce or coup de théâtre', in POMEPS Briefing no. 13. The full booklet is available at http://pomeps.org/wp-content/uploads/2012/08/POMEPS_BriefBooklet13_Egypt_Web.pdf.

26 For an attempt to place direct pressure on the SCC, see 'Egypt Court Halts All Work Amid Islamist "Pressure"', BBC, 2 December 2012, http://www.bbc.com/news/world-middle-east-20571718.

27 Patrick Kingsley, 'Egyptian Judge Sentences 720 Men to Death', *Guardian*, 28 April 2014, http://www.theguardian.com/world/2014/apr/28/egyptian-judge-sentences-720-men-death. Under Egyptian law, defendants sentenced in absentia – which may have been the majority – are automatically subject to retrial if they appear. These verdicts and sentences were issued in the full knowledge that most, if not all, were likely to be revised or reversed. The Grand Mufti, for example, formally rejected a death sentence passed on Mohammed Badie and urged the court to reconsider. See Lin Noueihed and Stephan Kalingy, 'Egypt's Mufti Rejected Brother Leader's Death Sentence, Court Urges Rethink', Reuters, 7 August 2014, http://www.reuters.com/article/2014/08/07/us-egypt-courts-badie-idUSKBN0G70ZJ20140807.

28 See David Kirkpatrick, 'Egyptian Judge Speaks Against Islamist Victory Before Presidential Runoff', *New York Times*, 7 June 2012, http://www.nytimes.com/2012/06/08/world/middleeast/egyptian-judge-speaks-against-islamist-victory-before-presidential-runoff.html?_r=0. Zend is an extremely controversial figure who led a demonstration by judges against Morsi and who was himself physically assaulted on one occasion. See 'Ahmed al-Zend, Anti-Morsy Judge, Assault Outside Judges Club', *Egypt Independent*, 23 December 2012, http://www.

egyptindependent.com/news/
ahmed-al-zend-anti-morsy-judge-
assaulted-outside-judges-club.

29 On 11 October, the State Council
announced that it had rejected a
proposed law granting university
presidents the right to fire faculty
members who took part in
demonstrations. See the Egyptian

Council of State Facebook page:
https://www.facebook.com/
pages/%D9%85%D8%AC%
D9%84%D8%B3-%D8%A7%D
9%84%D8%AF%D9%88%D9%
84%D8%A9-%D8%A7%D9%8
4%D9%85%D8%B5%D8%B1%
D9%8A-Egyptian-Council-of-
State/248414001977476.

CHAPTER THREE

The military

Dr Zeinab Abul-Magd

Less than one month after electing a new president in summer 2014, Egyptians awoke to dreadful news that the government had significantly reduced food and gas subsidies, leading to sudden increases in the prices of basic goods. Due to an acute budget deficit, President Abdel Fattah Al-Sisi, the former defence minister who had just swept elections, called on the nation to adopt austerity measures. To make things worse, he refused to respond to strikes calling for a minimum wage; a court decision subsequently sent striking employees into early retirement. Meanwhile, the president approved an increase of 8.3 billion Egyptian pounds (about US$1.2bn) to the military budget for 2014/15, followed by an increase of 4bn Egyptian pounds the following year (a total of US$1.7bn), and raised officers' pensions by about 25%. Furthermore, military contractors established a near monopoly over public construction projects. The army's business enterprises expanded – opening new filling stations, for example – and received new tax breaks. In a charitable move, the military decided to sell cheap produce from its expansive farms to needy citizens through its numerous retail outlets, and distributed free food boxes in villages and Cairo's slums.[1]

Sisi was the fourth officer to take off his uniform and govern the country since 1952. Before him, Gamal Abdel Nasser, Anwar Sadat and Hosni Mubarak had all formed authoritarian regimes, under which fellow officers enjoyed superior political and economic privileges entrenched within the state apparatus. This chapter argues that despite fundamental political and economic transformations, including a 'revolution' in 2011, the military as a semi-autonomous institution has managed to adapt to, and survive, these changes. At crucial moments of socialist, neoliberal or revolutionary transition, the military has maintained a hegemonic position in the state structure and maximised its economic profits, while deploying nationalistic rhetoric and constantly forging new socio-economic alliances. Evidently, the officers have successfully weathered the most recent wave of change, from which they emerged retaining their dominance. Nevertheless, this chapter poses questions about the ability of the Sisi regime to adapt to simmering discontent in such difficult post-revolutionary times, particularly because he has enacted incoherent economic policies unfavourable to the very socio-economic groups that elected him.

The chapter investigates the history and contemporary realities of Egypt's 'adaptable officers'[2] as they have adjusted to moments of fundamental transition. The first section briefly explores the socialist era under Nasser in the 1950s and 1960s, the open-door (*infitah*) years under Sadat in the 1970s, and the neoliberal transformations under Mubarak in the 1980s–2000s, analysing how the officers positioned themselves within these authoritarian orders. The chapter then explores the uprisings from 2011 until summer 2013, examining how the Supreme Council of the Armed Forces (SCAF) adapted to the revolutionary currents, and even profited economically and politically from them. Finally, it inquires into the current regime, focusing on Sisi's ultra-nationalistic rhetoric; the socio-economic alliances that he forged for electoral and populist support; the continuous increase in military business profits during his tenure; and his ambiguous economic policies that may potentially generate unrest among some of his most ardent supporters.

From socialism to neoliberalism, 1950s–2000s

Egypt's first military regime was born on 23 July 1952 when a group of young officers launched a coup, deposing the monarch and expelling the British colonial authorities. Only a few weeks afterwards, in response to long-standing demands from the poor, the ruling officers promulgated a land-reform law, which confiscated thousands of acres from the aristocracy and distributed them to impoverished peasants. Other measures soon followed that nationalised local and foreign industry. The army, led by Nasser as the country's first military president (1954–70), appointed itself as the 'vanguard of progress' and social justice in the newly independent nation.[3] After it officially adopted socialism in 1962, the state came to own all economic assets and built numerous public enterprises, while army officers installed themselves as the managers of these state-owned factories and companies. Corruption, mismanagement and failure proliferated throughout the public sector.

After a combination of a humiliating military defeat in 1967 and various economic failures, the army fell from grace politically. During the 1970s, Sadat – the second military president of the country (1970–81) – took radical steps to demilitarise the state. He marginalised officers from politics, increased the number of civilian technocrats in the cabinet and the bureaucracy, and radically reduced the number of military governors in provincial areas.[4] Moreover, the army's economic control over the public sector declined under Sadat's 'open door' policy, as he privatised parts of state-owned enterprises that officers had previously managed. To make things worse, as far as the army was concerned, Egypt signed a peace treaty with Israel in 1979, which reduced its role in politics – at least theoretically.

Nonetheless, the military managed to adjust, reviving its hegemonic status under Mubarak, the third military president of the country (1981–2011). A key institution in this process was the National Service Products Organisation (NSPO), which the defence ministry established as part of the 1979 peace agreement. The goal of the NSPO was to channel the energy of officers who were no longer needed for combat into economic development. Field Marshal Abd al-Halim Abu Ghazala, Mubarak's first defence minister and a member of his ruling National Democratic Party (NDP), transformed the NSPO into a business empire for civilian production and services. Abu Ghazala strongly believed that the liberalising policies of *infitah* should be applied not only to the Egyptian economy but to the military as well.[5] Throughout the 1980s, the NSPO and other military-affiliated bodies established chicken and fish farms, mechanised slaughterhouses, bakeries for subsidised bread, factories that produced frozen vegetables, pasta and textiles, and much more. They also built thousands of apartment buildings, bridges, roads, schools and hospitals for the government.[6]

Officers disappeared from movies and songs celebrating their heroism, as they forged a new discourse about their contribution to 'economic development' in the post-war era. To justify penetrating non-military economic realms, the army said that its civilian produce and services were mainly for its own self-sufficiency, national price control and the welfare of the poorer people. Abu Ghazala claimed to be helping the government with its five-year economic plan by using illiterate, working-class conscripts who were not 'medically, culturally, technically, or psychologically fit' for military service in civilian service instead – as free labour.[7]

When the age of accelerated neoliberalism arrived in Egypt in the 1990s and 2000s, the adaptable officers again made new adjustments and took immense advantage of the changes. They expanded their vast empire of profitable enterprises and restored considerable power to themselves, compensating for the losses they incurred under Sadat. While continuing in public to trumpet their patriotic contribution to economic development,[8] they switched their old socialist alliances from the working classes to the rising business elite and foreign capital in a market-economy milieu.

This was during a difficult period of 'defence conversion' in Egypt, when arms manufacturers had to switch to civilian goods. The process started in 1992 when Mubarak announced budget cuts and encouraged the army to convert to civilian production to compensate for the reduced military budget. The three main military-production conglomerates partially converted: the Ministry of Military Production (MoMP), the Arab Organisation for Industrialisation (AOI), and the NSPO. According to recent official statements, the MoMP owns eight manufacturing plants and 40% of their production is geared toward civilian markets, while the AOI owns 11 factories and companies, with 70% of production going to civilian markets. The NSPO engages only in civilian goods and services. Military conglomerates thus switched to producing chemicals, optics, plastics, fertilisers and mineral water, and created companies for mining, petroleum, cleaning and maintenance. They also produced pasta, luxury jeep cars, computers, engines, and water, sewage and gas pipes.[9] In addition, military corps constructed numerous hotels, wedding halls and gas stations, while reclaiming thousands of acres of desert land for commercial agriculture.

Military 'entrepreneurs' expanded even further in the 2000s, taking advantage of the accelerated pace of market reforms, led by Mubarak's son and NDP leader Gamal. The army started to invest in capitalist projects with a globalised orientation, such as heavy industries and export-oriented agriculture. For example, in 2004 the AOI purchased Semaf, the state-owned railway-wagon factory on the outskirts of Cairo, and in 2005 the MoMP opened a steel factory in Qaliubiyya. In 2010 the NSPO started building a cement factory in al-Arish in North Sinai; and the following year it finished building a complex for chemicals, including fertilisers, in Fayyum. The NSPO also invested in export-oriented farms in Mubarak's land-reclamation project, known as Toshka or 'New Valley', and created a transportation company in Aswan to ship the farms' commercial produce along the Nile. Furthermore, in addition to developing the regular road network, military companies also built toll highways in Upper Egypt,[10] from which they collected daily fees.

In preparation for Gamal's succession, Mubarak needed to coup-proof his regime. He did so by appointing an unprecedented number of retired officers to top administrative positions in almost every part of the bureaucratic apparatus and across the country. Consequently, the majority of provincial governors were retired army generals – 14 out of 26 governors in 2005. Those who did not make it to governor served as governors' chiefs-of-staff, directors of small towns, or heads of highly populated districts in Cairo. They ran key government authorities that controlled state land and urban development (including sea, river and land ports), the Suez Canal, foreign trade, tourism, investment, as well as public services (such as water and sewage, garbage collection and beautification). For example, the chairmen of the state authorities of the Red Sea, Alexandria, Damietta and Port Said seaports and Aswan's High Dam river port were all retired generals, as was the manager of the public Holding Company for Maritime and Land Transport – giving the military control of all means of public transportation in the country. The state-owned oil sector also became highly militarised, as retired generals were put in charge of natural gas and oil companies.[11]

During Field Marshal Muhammad Tantawi's tenure as defence minister and member of the state's public-sector privatisation committee, military entrepreneurs formed lucrative ties with local and international capital – especially Arabian Gulf partners. According to Shana Marshall and Joshua Stacher:

> The Kuwaiti group M. A. Kharafi and Sons … has joined the Egyptian military in a number of ventures, including the Arab Company for Computer Manufacturing, Egypt's only producer of computer hardware and laptops, in which Kharafi owns 71 percent of shares and the AOI and a Ministry of Military Production subsidiary each own 5 percent … The military and Kharafi also run an operation called Maxalto, which relies on technology from the German firm Schlumberger to manufacture smart cards.[12]

Whenever a new enterprise was launched, official statements from its military managers filled national newspapers, discussing how the project would work toward self-sufficiency to make the military less of a burden on the state budget, help the state with its development plans, serve the welfare of the masses by providing them with cheap goods and contribute to price control. However, the reality was different: the army were competitors in the neoliberal market, but with exceptional privileges. The army's untaxed, unaudited enterprises distorted the free market in their own interests rather than correcting it for the benefit of the masses. For instance, the aforementioned cement factory in al-Arish – erected on public land in collaboration with a Chinese company and using German technology – claims to help control prices, but the price of military cement was similar to that of other public and private factories, or sometimes higher. Similarly, the Semaf factory has not sold its products at affordable prices for the benefit of rail users – otherwise the Ministry of Transportation could have afforded to renew the railroad system and save the lives of hundreds who die in train accidents every year.[13]

Winning a revolution, 2011–13

In February 2011, after a sit-in that lasted 18 days, protesters in Tahrir Square celebrated ousting Mubarak and aborting his son's succession plan. The protesters had demanded not only an end to the Mubarak regime, but also to its destructive market transition, and had carried banners that called for social justice. Led by Tantawi, the SCAF immediately offered to run the country for a short transitional period of six months. Grateful for such support, the Egyptian masses chanted 'The army and the people are one hand' and state-owned media played national songs from Nasser's era. The SCAF stayed in power for 18 months before handing power to an elected president from the Muslim Brotherhood, Muhammad Morsi, in June 2012.

When the January 2011 uprising targeted the failed neoliberal regime of Mubarak, his son and their crony capitalist allies, the officers again quickly adapted to the new situation. After serving as Mubarak's defence minister for two decades, Tantawi abandoned the regime, as did serving and retired officers who had enjoyed economic and political influence. The military allied with wealthy Islamists and increased its hold over business and politics, despite prolonged protest and turmoil. Upon assuming power, the SCAF appointed two weak prime ministers, who signed letters of appointment for a large number of retired army generals and colonels in the state bureaucracy and the public sector. The SCAF also issued a law that granted army officers accused of corruption immunity from prosecution in civilian courts, including those who retired and occupied civilian offices.[14] In addition, the SCAF opened an industrial-chemicals complex producing fertilisers south of Cairo and a new cement factory in North Sinai. It also constructed new toll highways in Upper Egypt for profit.

The SCAF had a conspicuous marriage of convenience with the Brotherhood, based on power-sharing. After assuming power, the SCAF voluntarily adopted a democratic line and oversaw four elections: a referendum on a constitutional declaration drafted by a SCAF-nominated committee, which included Brotherhood leaders and was headed by an Islamist judge; two parliamentary elections; and one presidential election. In every election, the ballots were in favour of the Islamists – particularly the Brotherhood and the Salafis. At the referendum in March 2011, Islamists were instrumental in mobilising the masses to vote in favour of the SCAF's constitutional declaration, and the SCAF repaid the favour. The armed forces protected polling stations, but they allowed Islamists to violate electoral rules by conspicuously using religious slogans and distributing publications with religious signs at electoral commissions. In addition, civil-society organisations monitoring the elections recorded cases of vote-buying in exchange for food in rural and urban areas.[15]

The Brotherhood returned the favour. In June 2012, after Morsi had won the presidential election, he began his first national address by thanking the army. He saluted the Egyptian military and added: 'Only God knows how much love I have in my heart [for it]'.[16] Morsi maintained the privileged status of the army in the bureaucracy by hiring its officers as ministers, governors and other top administrators. In August 2012, he sacked Tantawi and replaced him with Sisi, after a terrorist attack in Sinai that killed 16 army conscripts. Rumours spread suggesting that Sisi was secretly a member of the Brotherhood, and to begin with he fully cooperated with Morsi's government.

The Brotherhood granted the military a semi-autonomous status in the constitution they hastily drafted and passed by popular referendum in December 2012. Article No. 197 shielded the military budget – including revenue from civilian businesses – from public scrutiny, and gave oversight to the National Defence Council, a government body that consisted mainly of officers appointed by the military. The legislature was obliged to consult the same council about any future laws relevant to the armed forces before they were issued. Furthermore, Article No. 195 stipulated that the defence minister should always be chosen from ranking officers; in other words, a civilian could not be appointed as minister of defence.[17]

The SCAF continued to expand its business empire during this period, as the Brotherhood-led government granted the military extensive advantages overstepping sound civil–military relations.[18] The Shura Council (Magles al-Shura, the upper house of the legislature), which was under Brotherhood control, helped the military expand its business empire in collaboration with Morsi's cabinet. The Shura Council's human-development committee transferred the property rights of a state-owned car factory to the MoMP.[19] The MoMP invested in assembling tablets and various ministries placed orders to buy thousands of these tablets without competitive public tenders.[20] In addition, the military acquired land to build shopping malls[21] and received a state permit to establish a medical school to train staff for its profitable hospitals that treated civilians.[22] Given that the budget of the army's civilian enterprises remained secret, the head of the state's Central Auditing Organisation complained that he had no access to the accounts of military-owned businesses.[23]

For many long months, Sisi was content to enjoy such advantages. He invited Morsi to military ceremonies, celebrating the graduation of new officers or the establishment of new military projects. However, the military eventually started to perceive the Brotherhood – a wealthy transnational movement – as a threat to national security, a fear that resonated in the Gulf states, which resented its ideological expansion and later supported its overthrow.

Besides severe economic underperformance and violence towards protests by the opposition, the Brotherhood was viewed as publicly supporting jihadist groups in and outside the country. During a celebration for the 1973 war victory, Morsi invited several jihadists who had been convicted of assassinating Sadat – considered to be the hero of that very war – to attend.[24] Two weeks before his ousting, Morsi attended a gathering with tens of thousands of Islamists from different factions at Cairo Stadium and implicitly backed their declaration of a 'jihad' in Syria. Without military pre-approval, he announced that the 'Egyptian people and army' would help free Syria.[25] Three weeks earlier, after an armed group in the Sinai peninsula had kidnapped seven soldiers, Morsi interfered against a planned military operation against the kidnappers, who eventually escaped without being identified.[26] Several former officers later asserted that the Brotherhood had facilitated the criminals' escape, and alleged that the Brotherhood and Hamas sponsored jihadists in Sinai.[27]

These incidents enabled Sisi to build a 'national consensus' around his hitherto obscure persona with the goal of confronting the Brotherhood. Since youth movements were essential to translate this consensus into action on the ground, the military covertly backed a Nasserist-leaning youth group that launched a campaign called Tamarod (Rebel) to collect signatures to impeach Morsi.[28]

On 3 July 2013 Sisi ousted Morsi and formed an interim coalition government, led by the head of the constitutional court. Oddly, he crafted pragmatic alliances that incorporated a wide political spectrum, including leftists, liberals and even Salafis. He also enlisted the Coptic Church to represent the nation's Christian minority, and al-Azhar as a representative of non-politicised Islam.

Cheerfully expressing their appreciation for the military's actions, the celebrating masses filled Tahrir Square, with posters of Nasser next to those of Sisi. The army's public-relations department funded the production of a song, *Tislam al-Ayadi*, which 'greeted the hands' of the soldiers who saved the nation, while invoking the 1973 war. The song quickly became so popular among Egyptians of all social classes that it is commonly played at weddings. This marked a new phase for the adaptable officers, who switched alliances once more, this time using practised nationalistic rhetoric to regain power.

Sisi versus malcontents

On the path to sweep presidential elections in 2014, Sisi sought the backing of various groups in society: mainly the business elite, but also workers in the public and private sectors, and middle-class women. Although the strategy worked initially, Sisi subsequently adopted economic policies that have displeased the very social groups that voted for him. Not only do his economic policies lack clear planning, but they are also incoherent regarding which economic model to follow. On the one hand, he imposes a strong role for the state and military in running the economy, and extends government support to the middle and lower classes, *à la* Nasser. On the other, he pursues market reforms by eliminating subsidies and stimulating investments from the business elite, following in Mubarak's footsteps. Wrapped in an ultra-nationalistic discourse, Sisi aspires to revive Nasser's socialist state under military control, and yet he is in dire need of local and foreign capital that only thrives in a liberalised market. These confused economic policies have not assuaged post-revolutionary discontent among his support base; on the contrary, unrest is evolving.

Shortly after removing Morsi, the interim government allied itself with the country's leftist groups, especially social democrats and Nasserists. Apparently, this alliance was to appease the working classes who were demanding the introduction of a minimum wage. The prime minister, Hazem al-Beblawi, was a member of the Egyptian Social Democratic Party and appointed ministers from a similar background. For example, the labour minister, Kamal Abu Eita, was a Nasserist leader of independent labour unions. The minister of social solidarity, Ahmad al-Burai, was also a strong supporter of such unions. However, this left-leaning cabinet conspicuously failed to pacify workers' strikes and resolve the long-standing minimum-wage dispute, ultimately leading to its resignation.[29] The interim government quickly switched allegiances again, as a cabinet led by Ibrahim Mehleb replaced leftist officials with either technocrats or liberals. This cabinet was not successful in assuaging labour protests either.

Before the presidential election, the interim government under Sisi appointed a committee of 50 public figures, many of them leftists, who drafted a new constitution that was confirmed by popular referendum in January 2014. Although its text introduced many progressive clauses relating to workers, women, youth and so on, it upheld the privileges the military had secured in the Brotherhood's constitution. Article No. 203 of the new constitution states that the military budget is to be listed as only one figure in the state budget and only the National Defence Council may discuss it. The same council should be consulted on any draft laws related to the armed forces. Article No. 201 stipulates that the defence minister must be a military officer, and Article No. 204 that civilians who attack military enterprises are to be tried in military courts. (This law was applied after a young citizen had a fight with a colonel in charge of running a military filling station and was sent to a military court.)

The interim government continued the practice of hiring a large number of retired officers to fill top government positions, which they kept after Sisi's election. For example, 15 governors of provinces are retired army generals. Other fellow retired officers are currently in charge of ports, including the Damietta, Alexandria, Port Said and Red Sea port authorities. The heads of the government authorities responsible for industrial and agricultural development, and land surveying, are all retired generals, as are the heads of state-owned holding companies for chemicals, land and sea transportation, and grain silos. After his election, Sisi appointed more fellow generals to key positions, such as the head of the subways and tunnels authority, and the maritime-navigation safety authority.

Furthermore, military contractors embarked on large public construction projects worth billions of Egyptian pounds without having to go through competitive and fair public tenders. To ease the process, the interim president Sisi promulgated Decree No. 48 in 2014, which amended the public bids and tenders law to allow the government to conclude agreements with contractors through 'direct allotment' in 'urgent' matters for construction projects of 10 million Egyptian pounds (US$140,000) or less. Thus the government hired military contractors to build or develop hospitals, bridges, roads, tunnels and social housing. A notable example is the Cairo–Alexandria toll road. According to official statements, between September and November 2013 alone, army entities were awarded public construction contracts worth around 7bn Egyptian pounds (more than US$1bn).[30] After Sisi was elected in August 2014, the head of the military engineers' authority stated that his corps was engaged in 850 public construction projects in fields as varied as transportation, affordable housing, education, health, sanitation services, government buildings and land reclamation. Around the same time, the military obtained 10,000 acres for land reclamation and commercial farming in the western desert, and 40,000 square metres to build four filling stations in Upper Egypt.[31]

Such economic hegemony has generated discontent among the business elite. During his presidential campaign, Sisi sought the support of influential business tycoons from the Mubarak era. Many of them backed him, especially those who own media networks, but others showed noticeable apathy. In April 2014, the head of the Federation of Egyptian Industries complained about the privileges accorded to military contractors in developing and administering toll roads, and insisted that the Cairo–Alexandria highway contract in particular was illegal.[32] Furthermore, one of the reasons that the turnout at the presidential election was so low[33] – which led the voting period to be extended over three days – was that owners of private-sector factories refused to give workers time off to vote.[34] A few weeks after his election, Sisi invited a large group of business leaders for a Ramadan iftar at the presidential palace, where he encouraged them to contribute to the country's development and promised to revise investment laws to stimulate more local and foreign capital.[35] Meanwhile, his new cabinet imposed a 10% tax on capital gains in the stock market in an attempt to boost state revenue.[36] It later cancelled the tax under pressure from the business community.[37]

As for workers, the situation has not improved. Protests have continued over the minimum wage and other financial rights.[38] During his campaign, Sisi appealed to workers for electoral support, and secured endorsements from the old labour unions previously affiliated with the NDP, as well as many of the newly formed independent unions.[39] Although Sisi's cabinet introduced a minimum wage, it was restricted to a minor raise for government employees and was not applied to workers at state-run holding companies or the private sector.[40] In a post-election statement, Sisi affirmed that he would not give in to labour protests and their 'sectoral demands', because the government does not have the resources. Labour unions raised objections and the statement caused widespread controversy.[41] Meanwhile, Sisi issued a series of laws to increase military pensions by a total of 25% in less than one year,[42] after they had already been raised by 15% under the SCAF in 2011 and by a further 15% under Morsi in 2012. Sisi also increased the military budget from around 31bn to 39bn Egyptian pounds (US$3.9bn to $US4.9bn) during FY2014/15, and to 43bn (more than US$5.1bn) in FY2015/16.[43]

As for middle-class women, whom Sisi has always addressed in his speeches and repeatedly appealed to for support, they have also faced financial crises at home. Sisi intensively targets women with an ultra-nationalistic message about their duties as wives and mothers of the nation, and has an appeal that reaches across social classes and age groups.[44] Immediately after the elections, however, he implemented a policy of austerity and the cabinet suddenly reduced food and gas subsidies in the middle of Ramadan, in an attempt to reduce the budget deficit. Special government smart cards were introduced that limited the number of loaves of subsidised bread people could buy each day.[45] And the government also raised the price of electricity and natural gas, which multiplied the cost of monthly bills.

Conclusion

Throughout the past six decades, the military has endured waves of fundamental transformation in the country's politics and economy, and maintained its hegemonic status within successive authoritarian regimes. It has quickly shifted socio-economic alliances and relied on nationalistic rhetoric to accumulate political privileges and create a business empire. Most recently, the military has survived revolutionary changes, even to emerge triumphantly above civilian actors and win back the presidency after briefly losing it. All the while, the military has projected an image of cohesion. By the time Sisi left his position as minister of defence, he had already hand-picked his successor and chiefs of corps from his close circle to ensure the loyalty of the commanders, and he pays occasional visits to cadets in military academies and holds regular 'cultural seminars' for young officers.

Nevertheless, during his first year in power, this most recent military president has applied ambiguous economic policies that have generated growing discontent among his supporters and socio-economic base. While he has continued to favour military enterprises with extensive business opportunities over the public and the private sectors, he has also attempted to introduce market reforms, including cutting subsidies, which negatively affect the livelihoods of the lower and middle classes. The regime has not fulfilled its promises to introduce a minimum wage for workers, alleviate farmers' debts, create job opportunities for young people, improve the lives of women and their families, and implement development projects in marginalised areas. Moreover, anticipated foreign capital and investments have stalled because of declining security and increasing terrorist attacks. It is not clear whether the military will manage to survive continuous, post-revolutionary unrest once more.

Notes

1   Salwa al-'Antari, 'al-Inhiyazat al-Ijtima'iyya li-l-Qrarat al-Iqtisadiyya', *Majallat al-Dimuqratiyya*, 29 September 2014; MENA, 'Muhafidh Qina: Takhsis 22 Alf kartuna Ramadaniyya li-Tawzi'iha 'ala al-Fuqara'', *al-Masry al-Youm*, 19 May 2015; Amani Abu al-Naga, 'al-Sisi: Lan Astati' Talbiyat Matlab Fi'awi Wahid...', *al-Shorouk*, 24 June 2014; Prime Minister's Decision No. 1455 of 2014, *al-Jarida al-Rasmiyya*, Issue no. 37, 11 September 2014; Rajab Jalal, 'Wazir al-Difa' Ya'fi 574 Munsha'a li-l-Jaysh min al-Dariba al-'Aqariyya', *al-Masry al-Youm*, 3 June 2015. The state budget is available at http://www.mof.gov.eg.

2   This term is inspired by Joshua Stacher's *Adaptable Autocrats: Regime Power in Egypt and Syria* (Palo Alto, CA: Stanford University Press, 2012).

3   See Gamal Abdel Nasser, *Falsafat al-Thawra* (Cairo: Bayt al-'Arab li-l-Tawthiq al-'Asri, 1996).

4   Ahmad Abd Allah (ed.), *al-Jaysh wa-l-Dimuqraitiyya fi Misr* (Cairo: Sina li-l-Nashr, 1990); Mark Cooper, 'The Demilitarization of the Egyptian Cabinet', *International Journal of Middle Eastern Studies*, vol. 14, no. 2, May 1982, pp. 208, 210.

5   Robert Springborg, *Mubarak's Egypt: Fragmentation of the Political Order* (London: Westview Press, 1989), p. 261.

6   See *Al-Malaff al-Watha'iqi lil-Mushir Muhammad 'Abd a-Halim Abu Ghazala* (Cairo: Markaz al-Ahram lil-Tanzim wal-Microfilm, 1981–89), Parts 2 and 3.

7   Abd Allah, *al-Jaysh wal-Dimuqraitiyya fi Misr*, pp. 96–9.

8   See, for example, General Jamal Mazlum, *al-Quwwat al-Musallaha wa-l-Tanmiya al-Iqtisadiyya* (Cairo: Markaz Dirasat al-Duwal al-Namiya, 1999).

9   For an overview of their civilian products and services, see the official websites of NSOP and AOI: http://www.nspo.com.eg and http://www.aoi.com.eg/aoiarab/index.html.

10 For more details, see Zeinab Abul-Magd, 'Time for a Civilian Handover', *Egypt Independent*, 1 April 2012, http://www.egyptindependent.com/opinion/time-civilian-handover.

11 See Zeinab Abul-Magd, 'The Egyptian Republic of Retired Generals', *Foreign Policy*, 8 May 2012, http://foreignpolicy.com/2012/05/08/the-egyptian-republic-of-retired-generals/; Zeinab Abul-Magd, 'Understanding SCAF', *Cairo Review of Global Affairs*, vol. 6, summer 2012.

12 Shana Marshall and Joshua Stacher, 'Egypt's Generals and Transnational Capital', *Middle East Report*, vol. 42, no. 262, spring 2012.

13 Khayr Raghib, 'Taqrir Hukumi: 82% min Khutut al-Sikak al-Hadidiyya Aqall Amanan', *al-Masry al-Youm*, 12 September 2010.

14 Decree of Law No. 45 of 2011.

15 Safa Surur, 'Taqrir Huquqi: Shira' Aswat wa-Bitaqat Dawwara wa Qudaha Yuwajjihun al-Nakhibin fi Awwal Ayyam al-Marhala al-Thalitha', *al-Masry al-Youm*, 3 January 2012, http://www.almasryalyoum.com/news/details/140434; Khalaf Ali Hasan and Mu'taz Nadi, 'Hurra Naziha': Ansar Mursi fi Qina

Yuwazi'un 'Zayt wa Sukkar' 'ala al-Nakhibin', *al-Masry al-Youm*, 24 May 2012, http://m.almasryalyoum.com/news/details/181086; 'Hurra Naziha: Mursi Yatasaddr Intihakat al-Yawm al-Awwal bi 57%', *El Badil*, 23 May 2012, http://elbadil.com/2012/05/23/47299/.

16 *Awwal Khitab li-l-Ra'is al-Misri al-Muntakhab Muhammed Morsi*, 24 June 2012, http://www.youtube.com/watch?v=pzs7R3lUeUQ.

17 For the full text of the constitution, see http://www.almasralyoum.com/node/1283056.

18 See Zeinab Abul-Magd, 'Chuck Hagel in Egypt's Economic Chaos', *Atlantic Council*, 29 April 2013, http://www.atlanticcouncil.org/blogs/egyptsource/chuck-hagel-in-egypt-s-economic-chaos; 'Egypt's Politics of Hidden Business Empires: the Brotherhood versus the Army', *Atlantic Council*, 5 October 2012, http://www.atlanticcouncil.org/blogs/egyptsource/egypt-s-politics-of-hidden-business-empires-the-brotherhood-versus-the-army.

19 Rami Nawwar and Kamil Kamil, 'Na'ib al-Nur Yaltaqi Wazir al-Intaj al-Harbi li-Bahth Tashghil al-Nsr li-l-Sayyarat', *al-Youm al-Sabi'*, 10 February 2013; Muhammad Abd al-'Ati, 'Tafa'ul bi-Intiqal Sharikat bi-Qita' al-'Amal li-l-Intaj al-Harbi wa-Tawaqqu'at bi-Najah al-Nasr li-l-Sayyarat', *al-Masry al-Youm*, 15 April 2013, http://www.almasralyoum.com/news/details/304338.

20 Khalid Hijazi, 'Iftitah Wazir al-Intaj al-Harbi wa-l-Ittisalat wa-Muhafiz al-Qaliyubiyya Khutut Intaj Awwal Tablit Masri', *al-Youm al-Sabi'*, 4 June 2013.

21 'Ammar al-Nisr, 'Bi-l-Suwar Mul Tijari Kabir li-Jihaz Khadamt al-Quwwat al-Musallaha bi-Blbis', *Sha'b Misr*, 18 March 2013, http://www.egyptianpeople.com/default_news.php?id=37703.

22 'Al-Shura Yuwafiq 'ala Insha' Kuliyyat Tibb Tabi'a li-l-Quwwat al-Musallaha', *al-Dustur*, 27 June 2013, http://www.dostor.org/227848.

23 'Ra'is al-Markazi li-l-Muhasabat: Ma 'Alaqat Qa'at Afrah a-Quwwat al-Musallaha bi-l-Amn al-Qawmi', *El Balad*, 4 November 2012, http://www.el-balad.com/303191.

24 'Jihan al-Sadat: Bakayt 'Indama Ihtafal Mursi bi-6 Uktubar fi Hudur Qatalat Zawji', *al-Masry al-Youm*, 28 September 2014, http://www.almasralyoum.com/news/details/533427.

25 Muhammad 'Ashur, 'Mursi Yasil Istad al-Qahira li-l-Musharaka fi Mu'tamar Nusrat Surya', *Elwatan*, 15 June 2013, http://www.elwatannews.com/news/details/201606.

26 'Mursi Mana' al-Hujum 'ala Musallahi Sina...' *al-Ahram*, 29 July 2013, http://gate.ahram.org.eg/UI/Front/Inner.aspx?NewsContentID=377716.

27 'Mu'asis al-Firqa 777: Ikhtitaf al-Junud Musalsal Batalahu al-Ikhwan wa-Hamas', *al-Arabiya*, 22 May 2013.

28 Ahmad Hamdi, '20 Mahatta fi Hayat Mahmud Badr Sani' Azmat al-Baskawit', *al-Masry al-Youm*, 20 December 2014, http://www.almasralyoum.com/news/details/606296.

29 Mansur Kamil and Daliya 'Uthman, 'Intifadat al-'Ummal

Tutih bi-Hukumat al-Biblawi', *al-Masry al-Youm*, 25 February 2014; http://today.almasryalyoum.com/article2.aspx?ArticleID=415315&IssueID=3152; Kamal 'Abbas, 'al-'Ummal Iktashafu Anna al-Hadd al-Adna lil-Ujur Wahm Siyasi', *al-Masry al-Youm*, 25 June 2014, http://www.almasryalyoum.com/news/details/470918.

30 Muhammad Sulayman, 'al-Jaysh Yahsul 'ala 'Uqud Muqawalat Hukumiyya bi-Qimat 7 Miliarat Junayh fi Shahr', *Masrawy*, 24 November 2013.

31 Muhammad Hasan, 'Ra'is al-Hay'a al-Handasiyya li-l-Ahram: 850 Mashru' Tusharik Fiha al-Quwwat al-Musallaha li-Khidamt al-Sha'b al-Misri', *al-Ahram*, 20 August 2014, http://www.ahram.org.eg/NewsQ/313622.aspx; Mahir Abu Nur, 'Mihlib Yatafaqqad 10 Alaf Faddan bi-l-Farafira Tastaslihum al-Quwwat al-Musallaha', *al-Youm al-Sabi'*, 14 September 2014.

32 Mahmud Sa'd Diyab, 'Ittihad al-Sina'at: Isnad Istighlal Misr Iskandariyya al-Sahrawi li-l-Jaysh Mukhalif li-l-Qanun', *al-Mal News*, 9 April 2014, http://www.almalnews.com/Pages/StoryDetails.aspx?ID=144940#.VfIQ1J3BzGc.

33 Turnout was 46% but after the third-day extension. Sisi had called for an 80% turnout. See Patrick Kingsley, 'Abdel Fatah al-Sisi sweeps to victory in Egyptian presidential election', *Guardian*, 29 May 2014, http://www.theguardian.com/world/2014/may/29/abdel-fatah-al-sisi-sweeps-victory-egyptian-election.

34 Ramy Muhassab, 'Talabat Rijal al-A'mal bi-Irsal al-'Ummal li-l-Taswit, Lamis al-Hadidi', *al-Wafd*, 26 May 2014.

35 Muhsin Salim, 'Tafasil Ijtima' al-Ra'is Ma'a Rijal al-'Amal', *al-Wafd*, 14 July 2014.

36 Hasan Subhi, 'Nanshur Tafasil Qanun al-Dara'ib 'ala al-Bursa al-Sadir al-Yawum bi-Qarar Ra'is al-Jumhuriyya', *Alborsa News*, 1 July 2014.

37 Muhammad Yahiya, 'Ba'd Ilgha' al-Dara'ib 'ala al-Bursa wa-Iqrar al-Ful Iradat Rijal al-A'mal Muntasira bi-Awamir Hukumiyya', *El-Badil*, 19 May 2015.

38 See, for example, a report compiled by the South Center for Rights on Labour in Upper Egypt: Rania Rabi', 'Ummal Sa'id Misr: Ihtijajat wa Ra'is Jadid', *Mada Masr*, 18 June 2014.

39 Rihab al-Shami, 'Hamlat Sisi Ta'rid Barnamajuhu al-Intikhabi 'ala 'Ummal Aswan', *Albawwaba News*, 4 May 2014, http://www.albawabhnews.com/554860; Siham Shawwada, 'Ittihamat Mutabadala bayna al-Niqabat al-Mustaqilla wa-Makatibiha al-Tanfidhiyya bi-Sabab Da'm Sisi', *al-Shorouk*, 9 May 2014, http://www.shorouknews.com/news/view.aspx?cdate=09052014&id=d45c2fba-a9cc-4814-bba9-2e7d04cfba95.

40 Shirif Mustafa, 'al-Khadamat al-Niqabiyya Tada' Ma'ayir Hadd 'Adil li-l-Ujur', *al-Tahrir*, 25 June 2014.

41 Iman 'Awf et al., 'Mawaqif Mutadariba min I'lan Sisi Rafd al-Matalib al-Fi'awiyya', *al-Mal*, 25 June 2014, http://www.almalnews.com/Pages/StoryDetails.aspx?ID=159165#.VTZERNKqpBc.

42 'Li-l-Marra al-Thalitha fi 'Ahdih al-Sisi Yuqarrir Ziyadat al-Ma'ashat al-'Askariyya bi-Nisbat 10%', CNN Arabic, 29 June 2015, http://arabic. cnn.com/middleeast/2015/06/29/ egypt-sisi-military-pension.

43 'Qarar Ra'is Jumhuriyya Misr al-'Arabiyya bi-l-Qanun Raqam 61 li-Sanat 2014 bi-Ziyadat al-Ma 'shat al-'Askariyya', al-Jarida al-Rasmiyya, Issue No. 26 Mukararr (H), 2 July 2014; Hisham al-Miyani, 'Mursi Ya'mur bi-Raf' 'Ilawat Ma'sahat al-Quwwat al-Musallaha li 15% Uswah bi-l-'Amilin fi al-Dawla', al-Ahram, 2 July 2012, http://gate.ahram.org.eg/ News/226974.aspx; Mustafa 'Id, 'Fi Awwal Muwazana li-l-Sisi Ziyadat al-Amwal al-Mukhasassa li-l-Ri'asa wa-l-Shurta wa-li-Difa', Masrawy, 11 September 2014.

44 Mahasin al-Sunusi, 'Sisi fi Mu'tamar 'al-Mar'a al-Misriyya': Ma Tiksarush bi-Khatri bi-Za'alkum minni', al-Masry al-Youm, 5 May 2014, http:// www.almasryalyoum.com/news/ details/440965; Jamal 'Abdu et al., 'Misr: al-Mar'a Taqud al-Intikhabat al-Ri'asiyya wa-Ghiyab al-Shabab', al-Qabas, 26 May 2014.

45 'Wazir al-Takhtit: Raf' As'ar al-Banzin wa-l-Sular wa-l-Kahraba' min Awwal Yuliyu', Amwal a-Ghadd, 28 June 2014, http://amwalalghad. com/index.php?option=com_con tent&view=article&id=142296&ca tid=15; Muhammad al-Sifi, 'Turuq al-Husul 'ala al-Khubz wa-l-Awarq al-Matluba fi al-Manzuma al-Jadida', al-Masry al-Youm, 4 July 2014, http://www.almasryalyoum. com/news/details/476201.

CHAPTER FOUR

The Muslim Brotherhood

Yasser El-Shimy

The Muslim Brotherhood has undergone a series of dizzying gyrations over the past three years that have offered it a historic opportunity to rule Egypt and posed a threat to its very existence. In a matter of months, it was transformed from a socio-religious group with a political wing into a political organisation with a socio-religious character. The movement jettisoned its long history of risk aversion, diving from one confrontation to another against an array of political adversaries, including the Egyptian military. The Brotherhood abandoned promises not to seek an electoral majority or to contest the presidency, and made the bet that winning elections was the only mandate it needed to be comfortably in charge. It shed allies, even within Islamist ranks, and made enemies. The movement cut deals with the old state, but sought to subvert it. The Brotherhood marginalised, and indeed antagonised, non-Islamist politicians and activists, but called on them to join its struggle once it had lost power. In doing so, the Brotherhood won it all and lost it all.

At the same time as the movement won and lost legislative and executive powers, the fortunes of Egypt's political transition itself oscillated violently back and forth. A pro-democracy revolt that began on 25 January 2011 culminated in an anti-democratic coup on 3 July 2013. What is more, large segments of the population, including those who had participated in the revolt, cheered on as the then-defence minister Abdel Fattah Al-Sisi declared an end to Muhammad Morsi's presidency, and embarked on a brutal crackdown against Islamists. That the Brotherhood's fate was tied to that of democratisation in Egypt is a reflection of the group's societal and political weight, and an outcome of the all-or-nothing approach adopted by political actors as they contested power in post-Mubarak Egypt.

This chapter sheds light on why the Brotherhood abandoned risk aversion and gradualism, and pursued seemingly unilateral, confrontational politics: firstly with the regime of Hosni Mubarak, then with its political opponents and finally with the army. The answers lie in the cost–benefit analysis the group has made at different intervals, seeing domestic, regional and international opportunities for its rise. It was either now or never. It also lay in the set-up of the organisation's decision-making structures. As internal power concentrated in the hands of a small group of hardliners, the group struggled to maintain its practice of seeking gradual, as opposed to abrupt or immediate, change. This turnabout would create rifts not only with non-Islamists apprehensive about the group's ostensible invincibility at the ballot box, but also with state institutions whose interests and prominence the Mubarak regime had long preserved, and which were loath to see them dispensed with by an alien caste of new rulers. The Brotherhood's seemingly endless quarrels did not stop with non-Islamist rivals; challengers from within the Islamist fold were equally troublesome. Salafis who had formerly been a guaranteed base of support developed their own party, al-Nour, and indeed became the biggest opposition party to the Brotherhood's Freedom and

Justice Party (FJP), winning approximately one-quarter of the seats in the 2012 legislature. The Salafis would exert pressure on the Brotherhood for further Islamisation, even as virtually everyone else pushed against.

Eventually, the Brotherhood found itself besieged by rivals from all directions, unable to translate its electoral triumphs into actual control over the state or the political sphere in general. Large crowds took to the streets, protesting over a host of issues, ranging from power cuts to Morsi's unilateralist approach, and demanded an early presidential election. The military, along with non-Islamist politicians and a cooperative judiciary, took power and discarded Egypt's short-lived democratic experiment. The sudden reversal in fortunes for the country's biggest socio-political organisation has had serious implications in relation to how it functions, its willingness to peacefully take part in post-coup politics and indeed what strategy it should pursue to regain what it lost.

A revolutionary opportunity for an evolutionary movement

In January 2011, the Brotherhood saw a historic political opportunity to end decades of repression and marginalisation. Its appetite for empowerment, and indeed self-confidence, would only increase with subsequent electoral successes. This represented a qualitative shift for an organisation that was not primarily political, and which had adopted a conciliatory approach to politics since a costly confrontation with the military rulers in the mid-1950s.

Gradualism, or the notion that the organisation should seek the Islamisation of society and the state over the long term, was a strategy developed in reaction to the state's debilitating crackdown on the movement in the 1950s and 1960s. It was also an ethos that the Brotherhood's founder, Hassan al-Banna, promoted. Indeed, the group historically emphasised the need for painstaking, long-term work by the members. According to its philosophy, a mixture of *daawa* (religious proselytising), charitable activities, and partial and gradual political participation would eventually lead to the establishment of a Muslim society and then the Muslim state. In the words of a prominent member: 'Al-Banna said in the 1940s that rule would seek us, and we would not seek it. The Brotherhood's ideology includes politics, but only after social change has been achieved.'[1] Another member elaborated further:

> Our doctrine does not rely on revolutions, but on pyramid-shape gradualism; it begins from the base, which is the individual and the family, and climbs up to society, which (once Islamised) engenders the Muslim state. We have already seen that dynamic at work with the 2011 parliament, where the Muslim society we have built voted for us in large numbers.[2]

Mere survival dictated pragmatic gradualism as well. The suppression of the Brotherhood by president Gamal Abdel Nasser was at times so severe that it nearly decimated the organisation. Many leaders were arrested or executed, while its networks of preaching and social services were largely severed.[3] Many members fled the country, mostly to conservative anti-Nasser Gulf monarchies.

The Brotherhood's leaders subsequently sought to preserve the group's very existence by coexisting with Egypt's military rulers. Anwar Sadat's pardoning of many members of the Brotherhood soon after he took office was taken as a gesture of goodwill. This did not mean that the Brotherhood had divorced itself from politics, but rather that at that time it had prioritised regrouping, reorganising and rebuilding.[4]

The Mubarak years saw the state slowly but surely withdraw from providing much-needed social and economic services to an overwhelmingly impoverished population, leading the Brotherhood to redouble its efforts to fill the vacuum. It established medical clinics, educational centres, business enterprises and charitable programmes.[5] As long as the Brotherhood recognised its political restrictions, the government tolerated this parallel state because it did not wish to carry out these duties or incur the expense. The Brotherhood continued to participate in parliamentary elections, university student unions and professional syndicates/labour unions. Although its participation was for the most part limited, it indicated a willingness to work within the system rather than against it.[6]

The group walked a thin line between its dual role as the country's biggest opposition party after the 2005 parliamentary elections, and its long-standing desire to avoid a clash with the Mubarak regime. Unlike activist groups such as Kefaya and 6 April,[7] the Brotherhood refrained from taking to the streets and opted instead to confine its grievances to the sphere of formal politics. This approach demonstrated the movement's inclination to reform, rather than confront, the regime. It also reflected concern about being dragged by secular groups into a fight whose repercussions the Islamists would disproportionately have to bear.[8]

However, in 2011 the Brotherhood had no choice but to join the uprising. Not only did its youth base show a rare moment of defiance by taking part in the protests against orders, but since the 2005 parliamentary elections the regime had systematically blocked all channels of peaceful political participation open to it.[9] Mubarak's purported scheme for his son Gamal to succeed him had prompted the regime to actively root out any sources of opposition. Many Brotherhood leaders, including powerful Deputy-General Guide Khairat al-Shater, became targets of a widening crackdown as well.

The leadership concluded that the lesson from this setback was that the group's Islamic project would only come about if it achieved power or succeeded in neutralising the state's repressive policies:[10] 'By 2010, we had realised all legitimate channels for change have been closed shut. The succession plan [from Mubarak to his son Gamal] was underway, and so there was no alternative to revolting.'[11] Protests that young non-Islamist activists initially led presented the Brotherhood with an immediate opening: it could ride the tide of mass popular anger at Mubarak's rule to extract political concessions and open up further space for its activities outside politics.[12]

In February 2011, as the transition began, the Brotherhood realised that its chance to rule Egypt was either now or never for a number of reasons. Firstly, the uprising's outcome far exceeded the Brotherhood's expectations: Mubarak had left office, and the generals who took power, the Supreme Council of the Armed Forces (SCAF), allowed the legalisation of political parties, including the Brotherhood's FJP. Secondly, the group grew in confidence, with a series of electoral victories: in March 2011 in a referendum to amend the 1971 constitution, and at parliamentary elections the following December; and the following year at the presidential election in May–June and a second constitutional referendum in December.[13] These results convinced the Brotherhood that it enjoyed the solid backing of the majority of Egyptians, further tempting it to compete for and accrue more power. Finally, the movement sought to capitalise on changes elsewhere in the region, where old autocrats were falling, and Islamists were poised to succeed them. Better yet, the United States appeared to sanction, or at least not to oppose, the Islamists' rise, and regional powerhouse Qatar offered funding and favourable media coverage through Al-Jazeera. It seemed like now or never.

There were salient risks for inaction as well. The Brotherhood feared a return of the Mubarak old guard, either through the ballot box or by judicial fiat. The FJP attempted and failed to build an electoral coalition with non-Islamist parties to compete against the *feloul*, remnants of the old regime, in the 2011–12 parliamentary elections. The Brotherhood felt, perhaps self-servingly, that if it stood by its earlier commitment not to seek more than half the seats, it would provide an opening for the old guard to crush disorganised and inexperienced secular parties.[14] Similarly, when it seemed likely that the military would push the Supreme Constitutional Court (SCC) to dissolve the legislature because of differences with the FJP over forming a cabinet, the Brotherhood responded daringly by nominating not one but two candidates for the presidency. The Brotherhood's post-2011 actions departed its gradualist tendencies. Sensing opportunities and fearing risks of inaction, the group set itself on a collision path with state institutions, particularly the military.

One against all

On their way to power, and also when in power, the Brotherhood's approach was characterised by a mistrust of other political actors, a willingness to take risks and recourse to identity politics (Islamist vs secular, Muslim vs Copt). It defaulted to truculent, confrontational politics at times of crises. The movement failed to build coalitions with pro-democracy parties, attempted to curtail the powers of state institutions and sought to place its members in the highest positions of power. Even internally, the Brotherhood's leadership demanded near-complete acquiescence to its directives, not only from members, but also from the FJP and Morsi himself.[15] After Morsi appeared unable to handle the growing opposition that followed his constitutional declaration in November 2012, which in effect banned judicial review of presidential decrees,[16] Shater moved to assume a leading position in presidential decisions. The leadership vetoed any conciliatory gestures by the beleaguered president, warning him against showing weakness.[17] These actions reinforced its detractors' apprehensions about power-sharing, and the perception that the FJP and Morsi were little more than tools in the hands of the Brotherhood's leadership.

This approach was the outcome of many factors, including the Brotherhood's tradition of secretive decision-making, which had emerged as a coping mechanism against the state's successive crackdowns. Influential leaders in the Guidance Bureau (the Brotherhood's highest executive body), such as Mohammed Badie (the General Guide), Shater (Badie's deputy), Mahmoud Ezzat and others, had spent at least part of their lives either in prison or in hiding. They had come to value insularity and secrecy as being indispensable to the movement's long-term survival. The ascendancy of this group, at the expense of the so-called reformists, would lead to growing intolerance of internal opposition and an appetite for taking risks.[18]

Following the breakdown of the Mubarak regime, the leadership's tolerance of the reformists' dissent plummeted to a nadir. Abdel Moneim Aboul Fotouh, a former Guidance Bureau member, was expelled for going against the wishes of the leadership, having declared shortly after the 2011 uprising that he would be running for president.[19] This high-profile dismissal served as a stern warning that all members, however senior, must abide by the leadership's instructions. The post-revolutionary atmosphere had initially tempted some members to openly express their desire for the group to become more open to other political actors, but that trend quickly disappeared as the pro-discipline faction in the leadership (*tanzimyeen*) systematically eliminated critics.[20] The defections and dismissals of reformist leaders (*islahiyeen*), and the Brotherhood's subsequent battles with their political rivals, increased the power of – and indeed support for – the *tanzimyeen*. Authority became more concentrated in the hands of the latter, leading the remaining 'reformists' to either quit the organisation or become more hawkish themselves. Talk of reforming internal statutes to make the Brotherhood more democratic and more inclusive of the youth steadily quietened down, especially given the group's lack of structural mechanisms for internal change.[21] The reformists had already lost a number of internal elections as the organisation's constituency had grown more rural and conservative over the previous three decades.[22]

To all intents and purposes, the *tanzimyeen* had practically removed challengers to their influence within the group and tightened their grip on its various offices and levers of power.[23] The Guidance Bureau had become more harmonious, and was confident in its ability to impose internal discipline. The organisational paradigm the *tanzimyeen* favoured – closed, hierarchical and somewhat authoritarian in its culture – dominated, whereas the culture of reform, especially among urban youth, sat on the margins. This transformation had political implications, as the Brotherhood became ever more distrustful of outsiders and insistent about maintaining internal discipline, as well as more unilateral in policy decisions.

The leadership also benefited from the Brotherhood's controversial foray into politics. The *tanzimyeen* did not hesitate to harness the group's enormous reservoir of resources and infrastructure towards achieving political dominance in Egypt. It pushed for active participation in the political process to 'assume a historical responsibility of guiding Egypt after the fall of Mubarak's regime'.[24] While the Brotherhood was far from unified in this respect, the momentous decision came about when the *tanzimyeen* lobbied their peers to nominate a presidential candidate. Many members of the group's Advisory Council refused to vote in favour of a decision they believed went back on earlier promises the Brotherhood had made and was full of risks,[25] such as alienating supporters, losing credibility or stirring up conflict with other political parties. In the event, the vote was so close that it had to be held twice, which allowed the *tanzimyeen* to persuade more members to vote their way the second time.[26]

Nevertheless, the decision was made in the *tanzimyeen's* favour, and they made a risky bet on their odds to win the presidential elections. The election results in both rounds were so close they left the leadership either in denial[27] or dumbfounded.[28] Ultimately, however, Morsi went on to win the presidential election, and like the preceding parliamentary victory, this enhanced the internal credibility of the Brotherhood's leadership. As one member put it at the time: 'As long as we are winning one election after another, why should the group engage in self-criticism or challenge those calling the shots? They are delivering'.[29]

Indeed, Morsi's very close victory did not end the *tanzimyeen's* penchant for unilateralism or risk-taking.[30] The group's leadership was privately dismayed by Morsi's overtures to non-Islamists to join his administration and cabinet. When Morsi's relations with non-Islamists deteriorated following his November 2012 constitutional declaration, the leadership put even more pressure on him to appoint Brotherhood members to the higher echelons of government. The leadership perceived growing challenges to the president and regarded chants of 'Down with the rule of the General Guide' by non-Islamists as part of a conspiracy to topple Morsi and circumscribe the influence of the Brotherhood. In reaction, they pressed the Islamist-majority Constituent Assembly to ignore a boycott by non-Islamists and vote on a constitutional draft that lacked broad agreement. Morsi subsequently put the constitution to a referendum and it was accepted. Once passed by a near two-thirds majority,[31] the leadership of the Brotherhood then 'recommended' a number of candidates for ministerial portfolios for Morsi's consideration.[32]

The sense of being rejected by others, coupled with the ability to win electoral contests, served to solidify cohesion inside the movement. But by the end of 2012, many non-Islamist politicians, notably under the auspices of the National Salvation Front (NSF), an opposition coalition, were openly questioning Morsi's legitimacy as president. This escalation, combined with the NSF's unwillingness to discuss contentious issues with Morsi in person, further convinced the Brotherhood that it was threatened by an intransigent opposition that was agitating for another revolt – or a coup. A member, who used to be critical of the *tanzimyeen*, changed his mind after the constitutional battle: 'With the kinds of attacks I have seen coming from the secularists against Morsi and the Brotherhood, I had to side with my tribe. We stand together or we fall together.'[33]

Another unfortunate tactic often deployed by the group's leadership was to heighten sectarian discourse at times of pressure. It openly complained about the alleged role of the new Coptic Pope Tawadros II in fomenting anti-Morsi protests[34] and siding with political rivals.[35] Ideological and sectarian ruptures reached a crescendo in the lead-up to, and after, Morsi's ouster.[36] Several churches, particularly in religiously divided Upper Egypt, were torched or vandalised when security forces lethally dispersed the pro-Morsi sit-in in Rabaa al-Adawiya in August 2013.[37]

And yet, as seemingly belligerent as the Brotherhood's tone and actions were, they betrayed more a sense of besiegement and insecurity than triumphant arrogance. Ironically, members feared that, unless they won all electoral contests and concentrated power in their own hands, they would suffer terrible repression akin to that experienced in the 1950s and 1960s. In retrospect, their fears appear to have been reasonable, even sanguine. The Brotherhood's electoral victories have been wholly rolled back as of 2015. The March 2011 referendum, which the movement supported, was rendered virtually void by the SCAF's first constitutional declaration[38] in 2011. The parliamentary elections from late November 2011–January 2012 produced an Islamist-majority legislature, which then saw its authority restricted by the SCAF, and a few months after its election, the lower house was abruptly dissolved by the SCC.[39] The prospect of a Morsi presidency drove the SCAF to issue a last-minute 'constitutional declaration' in June 2012 that effectively handed some executive and all legislative powers to the generals at the expense of the incoming president. Morsi faced protests from the opposition and strikes from many state organs unwilling to cooperate with him, most notably the judiciary and the police.

When the Brotherhood sought to steamroll past what it considered to be an obstructionist opposition by calling for a vote in December 2012 on the draft constitution, notable opposition figures called the outcome, which was in favour of the 'yes' vote, illegitimate.[40] Finally, on 3 July, the military, the judiciary and the non-Islamist opposition would all collaborate to overthrow the president after only a year in office. All of these developments served to further convince the Brotherhood's leadership that the threat it faced was 'existential', and that its battle was inherently zero-sum.[41] The Brotherhood was determined not to blink first, no matter what the consequences. In doing so, Egyptian politics succumbed to the calamitous dynamics of a self-fulfilling prophecy.

The state is the enemy; long live the state!

The Brotherhood did not mind political opposition, because it believed it could win nearly any election it entered. State institutions constituted the biggest threat to the movement, having previously faced persecution at the hands of the military, the police and even the judiciary. During its year in power, the Brotherhood therefore attempted to neutralise these threats, by means of cooperation, co-optation or confrontation, none of which succeeded in diminishing the animosity these institutions showed towards the Brotherhood, or giving the movement the upper hand. Ironically, in many cases the marriage of the old state with the new Islamist political elite was mutually beneficial, enabling officers and judges to eschew demands for overhauls, accountability and reform that non-Islamist parties were demanding. The Brotherhood, for its part, did not press for radical change, seeking merely to take over the reins of the state from Mubarak's party. Yet as modest as the Brotherhood's demands for change were, the state institutions met them with fierce resistance, deeply suspicious of Islamists and determined to protect their own interests and prerogatives.[42]

When members of these institutions cooperated, they were rewarded personally, by way of promotions, and institutionally, by preserving long-standing interests. When they opted for a clash, a clash they were handed. Ultimately, the Brotherhood's leaders perceived the so-called 'deep state', of which the anti-Islamist security sector is a main pillar, to be the most cumbersome obstacle to their rule. For a brief period, it appeared that a detente was possible. When anti-government protests took a violent turn in January 2013, Morsi went out of his way to defend the 'deep state' in its use of force.[43] Shortly afterwards, the police became more involved in confronting riots near the presidential palace, as well as FJP headquarters and other Brotherhood-affiliated premises. This rapprochement soon unravelled. As the Brotherhood lurched from one damaging political stand-off to another, bureaucrats, officers and judges became ever more convinced of the movement's unilateral tendencies – and its vulnerability.

For the Brotherhood, the hostile bureaucracy undermined Morsi's ability to govern and, by extension, the credibility of the movement itself.[44] Morsi was pressured into appointing Brotherhood members to government positions with the eventual aim of controlling the state apparatus. As one member acknowledged:

> Some appointments of Brotherhood members have been made beneath the ministerial levels. Prime Minister Hesham Qandil has not been very cooperative on this, but we are building up cadres to monitor the corrupt practices of the bureaucracy, and become ready to take over at some stage in the future.[45] This was part of a concerted strategy to tame the seemingly rogue state institutions: firstly, by reshuffling the leadership of the defence and interior ministries in August and December 2012; secondly, by appointing a member of the Brotherhood as a 'second-in-command', in governorships and other ministries; or, finally, by simply placing a member of the Brotherhood to a top position – at the transportation, supply and planning ministries, for example.[46]

The army

In the immediate aftermath of the revolution, the military and the Brotherhood shared an interest in bringing calm to the streets – the army so that the state institutions would not give way, and the Brotherhood so that it could win elections. Both entities defended institutional continuity and social order against revolutionary dynamics agitating for radical change.[47] The March 2011 constitutional amendments were in a way the crowning achievement of that understanding.[48] The military hoped that, by reaching an understanding with the Brotherhood, street mobilisation would end, and revolutionary fervour would dissipate. For the Brotherhood, the SCAF was supposed to perform a principal task: to enable the transfer of power to elected civilians.

This tentative understanding came undone due to many factors, including non-Islamist groups continuing to protest, which highlighted the Brotherhood's lack of control over street action. Additionally, the SCAF balked at the prospect of Islamist-dominated politics and sought to balance them. The military took a series of extraordinary steps that antagonised the Brotherhood, such as its unsuccessful attempt to issue 'supra-constitutional principles' in November 2011, the dissolution of the parliament, disqualifying Shater's candidacy for president, proclaiming a constitutional declaration on the eve of Morsi's election that deprived the executive of many of its important powers and, finally, publicly blocking Morsi's July 2012 decision to reinstate parliament.

These measures showed the Brotherhood that the SCAF was going to be a thorn in its side, no matter how many elections it won. In August 2012, Morsi dismissed the SCAF and annulled its constitutional declarations. He had hoped to replace the recalcitrant ageing leadership with a malleable cadre of young officers, including Sisi, believed by some to have Islamist sympathies. Rather than seeking to subjugate the army, Morsi offered younger officers access to the upper echelons of authority as long as they refrained from meddling in political affairs.

This modus vivendi allowed Morsi to adopt a more assertive domestic policy, but tempted him to go too far. His brash

announcement of the November 2012 constitutional declaration prompted massive protests outside the presidential
palace, which neither the police nor the army were willing to
confront on his behalf. By announcing a national referendum
on a deeply contentious constitutional draft, Morsi escalated
the crisis, angering many army generals:

> As an army, we have decided to remain out of politics,
> but we are citizens with families who are not immune
> to the effects of what's going on ... the ruling party
> should learn the way people ought to be governed.
> It is about how the constitution/social contract is
> produced. You can't have one faction [the Islamists]
> write the constitution.[49]

The relationship showed signs of fraying when the army's
leadership unexpectedly invited political leaders from all sides
to a meeting hosted by the defence minister, after the president's own invitation went unanswered.[50] As clashes between
the Brotherhood and the opposition escalated, some opposition
members called on the military to step in and depose Morsi. The
army subsequently issued a statement emphasising its commitment to the legal legitimacy of the elected president. In reality, the
military, seeing the weakness of the president and the persistence
of political turmoil and polarisation, had decided to take matters
into its own hands.[51] The Brotherhood, however, remained
naively certain of the army's loyalty until the last moment.[52]

When mass protests took place on 30 June 2013, the army's
leadership issued a 48-hour ultimatum to the president to
find a solution to the political crisis, or else the military would
impose its own 'road map'.[53] On 3 July, Sisi announced the
removal of Morsi and the appointment of the head of the SCC,
Judge Adly Mansour, in his stead.

The police and the judiciary

As with the army, Morsi did not seek a confrontation with the police force. Aware of the country's lack of security following the 2011 uprising, he dismissed revolutionary demands to reform the interior ministry. He even went so far as to suggest the 'police is in its [the revolution's] heart'.[54] He replaced the interior minister with another police general, and ordered pay raises for all police officers. None of these overtures were positively received, however.[55] On several occasions when protesters attacked FJP and Brotherhood offices, the police stood idly by. Officers reportedly even helped protesters storm the Brotherhood's headquarters in the Cairo district of Moqattam in December 2012.[56] Many police officers later joined the 30 June protests in uniform. After the coup, they arrested Brotherhood members en masse, and engaged in lethal confrontations with protesters on an almost weekly basis.

Arguably, no single institution has been as effective in undermining Morsi's presidency, and the Brotherhood's rise to power in general, as the judiciary. Not only did the SCC dissolve both chambers of the legislature and publicly oppose the president's decree to reinstate them, but it was also reportedly on its way to disbanding the Constituent Assembly. The judiciary impeded parliamentary elections in 2013, calling every draft electoral law sent before it for review unconstitutional. Even lower courts would make rulings on matters historically beyond their authority, such as the legality of individual presidential decisions. Judges, incensed by Morsi's constitutional declaration that immunised presidential decrees from their review, organised a far-reaching boycott that forced the referendum on the new constitution to take place in several stages.

Morsi tried and failed to control the judicial branch by appointing an Islamist-leaning justice minister and new prosecutor-general. When the military suspended the constitution and removed the elected president on 3 July, the SCC stood firmly behind the decision, with its top judge anointed as interim president. Later, Brotherhood members would receive harsh sentences for protesting against the coup, including mass death sentences handed down without even hearing the defendants' cases.[57]

All in all, state institutions worked to foil the Brotherhood's rise to power and ultimately succeeded. Their hostility to the Islamist group, whose ascendancy put their interests and authority in jeopardy, evolved into vindictiveness, as they unrelentingly repressed the group's members and supporters.

The Brotherhood survives the coup

To its loyal followers, the Brotherhood's leadership style of confrontational, divisive politics was initially validated by a series of unprecedented electoral victories, and then by the coup itself. The coup came to be seen as the fulfilment of the wide-ranging plot against the Brotherhood that the hawkish leadership had warned of.

Almost as soon as Morsi was elected president, Brotherhood members spoke of their fears of a conspiracy against him that included the pro-revolution opposition, remnants of the Mubarak regime and the United Arab Emirates.[58] This constant sense of being threatened ensured cohesion and vigilance in trusting the hierarchical leadership. Even relatively moderate voices within the movement, such as Mohammed al-Beltagy and Essam al-Erian, increasingly echoed the hawkish line of the *tanzimyeen*. Relations between the leadership and the base were seriously tested in the aftermath of the coup, when the army shut down pro-Morsi media channels and proceeded to arrest and kill thousands of the group's members and supporters.[59] The Brotherhood's leadership reacted defiantly, and in a manner meant to preserve the movement's cohesion, even if it was at the expense of their erstwhile political gains. This foiled the authorities' goal of dividing the Brotherhood, by enticing moderates to abandon the leadership and form a docile new entity.[60]

The leaders recognised early on that the coup was a watershed moment; they could either bow down to the popularly backed army takeover, or they could go down fighting. They opted to fight, because to do otherwise would have confirmed their critics' accusations: that their political approach was too risky, their governance incompetent and their credibility tarnished. For a group that until recently had refused to entertain the prospect of ever losing a free election, it faced genuine and widespread popular exasperation, as well as hostile armed forces.[61]

The Brotherhood adopted almost immediately an apocalyptic discourse stressing that this was a fight over the identity of the country – Islamic or not – and over the type of government – civilian or military. While the Brotherhood drew heavily on religious discourse with a theme song called 'Egypt is Islamic', it concurrently spoke of legitimacy, democracy and human rights, seeking to appeal not only to Egyptians, but also to an international audience. As one member of the Brotherhood put it: 'This is a clash of legitimacies between [19]52 [the date of Nasser's coup] and 25 January [the date of the revolt]. We cannot allow the military to rule again.'[62] Internally, members were urged to rally, despite the mounting risks, because the very survival of the movement was at stake.[63] On the ground, the Brotherhood's strategy was to mobilise pro-Morsi protests throughout the country and hold onto the Rabaa Square sit-in to show that 30 June was not truly a revolution. The show of force was indeed spectacular, as rallies unfolded from Marsa Matrouh to Sinai and from Alexandria to Aswan. Rabaa Square was filled with tens of thousands of supporters.

The FJP declined invitations to take part in discussions to come up with a post-Morsi road map, and rejected any political solution that did not entail the reinstatement of Morsi and the constitution. Meanwhile, leaders were either rounded up and sent to jail or went into hiding. The narrative they articulated was unequivocal: the military overthrew the first democratically elected president, secularists cheered on the brutal crackdown against their Islamist opponents, and the Brotherhood's leaders were once again paying a hefty price for taking a principled position against the coup. It revived the memories of the 'plight' of the 1950s and 1960s, when the group faced similarly adverse circumstances. More than ever, the group encountered an existential threat that necessitated absolute cohesion and entailed sacrifices – both for the sake of the Brotherhood and religion itself.

As the new authorities consolidated their power, violently quelling protests and dispersing sit-ins (such as infamously the murder of almost 1,000 people in Rabaa Square),[64] and arresting supporters en masse, members were still asked to protest on a weekly basis to show the justice of their cause and undermine the army's claim to be acting in accordance with popular will. Many lost their lives, while others became more socially isolated, were sentenced to lengthy prison sentences (over 41,000) and had their businesses and charitable activities suspended. The main solace for members was that if even senior leaders such as Badie, Shater and Morsi 'sacrificed themselves for the cause of [preserving] legitimacy, we should too'.[65] The notion of 'plight' that inhabited the Brotherhood's philosophy in the 1950s and 1960s was revived to instil a sense of historical responsibility in the current generation. They are expected to persevere in the face of adversity and await the divine promise of eventual triumph.[66] This narrative shuts the door on attempts at introspection or soul-searching, thus preserving the leadership's position within the organisation and ensuring discipline does not break down.

As the crackdown broadened with time and operating inside Egypt became next to impossible, the leadership reportedly reverted to leaders who had fled, such as Mahmoud Ezzat, and members based in London, Istanbul and Doha. The crackdown succeeded in severing much of the communication within the organisation; hence, the calls by Brotherhood and FJP members appealing on Al-Jazeera for supporters to become 'creative' in opposing the coup. This reflects lack of direct lines of communication within the organisation, as well as an admission of the failure of commonly used methods, such as rallies.

The extreme repression experienced by the Brotherhood had the unfortunate effect of pushing them towards a greater acceptance of the use of violence to accomplish political goals. Badie's famous message that 'our peacefulness is stronger than their bullets' ultimately gave way to calls for revenge against the police. Leaders would eventually introduce a laboured interpretation of Badie's motto by saying that peacefulness permitted everything short of firing bullets.[67] Younger members increasingly used Molotov cocktails to set fire to police stations and vehicles. Although the government branded the Brotherhood a terrorist organisation in December 2013, it has failed thus far to produce any concrete evidence linking the group to the series of lethal attacks against security forces since July 2013. More radical groups such as Ansar Bayt al-Maqdis have claimed responsibility for such attacks. More recently, youth factions have reportedly split from the Brotherhood, frustrated with their leaders' reluctance to use violence against security forces, and sworn allegiance to the Islamic State of Iraq and al-Sham.[68]

The radicalisation of youth groups within the Brotherhood imposes constraints on the ability of exiled leaders to take measures to de-escalate the situation or reconcile the movement with the current authorities. A rapprochement with Sisi would mean that the sacrifices thousands of members offered were ultimately pointless. This is why the Brotherhood is unlikely to seek reconciliation in the foreseeable future. Instead, it is likely to remain a spoiler, working relentlessly to destabilise Sisi's term in office with protests and acts of economic sabotage. It has calculated that when (not if) public anger rises due to rapidly worsening economic conditions, the military will consider Sisi's hardline approach too costly and a liability on the country's ability to move forward. The Brotherhood hopes for – and is working towards – another coup;[69] this time, a counter-coup.

It is too soon to tell if the movement will survive this plight intact, but for now, at least, it lives on to fight another day, convinced of the righteousness of its cause. As one member remarked: 'We do not make our calculations for weeks or months, but for years and decades. We have a long-term project, and we will outlive our rivals.'[70] It is clear, however, that the Brotherhood has failed to convince most other groups that its members' sacrifices and struggles have been for the sake of country or democracy rather than for the sake of the Brotherhood itself. As the group continues to internally debate who is worthy of leading – the old guard or younger leaders – and if it should seek an accommodation or confrontation with the authorities, the sheer weight of the relentless crackdown is bound to show. Not unlike Jordan, Egypt too may soon have more than one Brotherhood. Indeed, this may already be the case.

Notes

1 Interview with a founding member of the Freedom and Justice Party, Cairo, October 2012.

2 Interview with Ossama Soliman, a former FJP member of parliament, Damanhour, November 2012.

3 This crackdown left such an indelible memory in the collective conscience of the group that Morsi referred to it in his informal inauguration speech in Tahrir Square. 'Mohammed Morsi yu'adi al-qasam fi midan al-Tahrir: al-khitab al-kamil', 1 July 2012, http://www.youtube.com/watch?v=LGoxgvkcLYo.

4 The men who championed this ambitious effort, the *tanzimyeen*, have placed great emphasis on the principles of discreetness, suspicion toward outsiders, discipline, hierarchy and obedience as the most desirable values and practices organisationally. Reformists, on the other hand, sought in the 1990s and 2000s to make the group less rigid, and more transparent, open to collaborating with outsiders, as well as democratic and decentralised. The *tanzimyeen* perceive the reformists' demands as coming out of the luxury of not having lived through the brutal experience of the government crackdown in the 1950s and 1960s.

5 Much of this was made possible, ironically, by the sometimes forced migration of Muslim Brothers to the Gulf, where they went on to make large fortunes.

6 The two instances in which the Brotherhood heavily participated in street protests were in 2000, when the Palestinian intifada broke out, and in 2003, during the US-led invasion of Iraq. Street politics was confined to foreign-policy issues.

7 Kifaya (Enough) was founded to oppose Mubarak's plan in 2005 to run for yet another term in office. 6 April was a pro-labour, anti-Mubarak youth group that in 2008 helped organise the largest strike to take place in Egypt under Mubarak, in the industrial town of al-Mahalla al-Kubra.

8 Many non-Islamists point to this behaviour as indicative of the Brotherhood's lack of 'revolutionary credentials', arguing the Brotherhood lacked the courage to tackle the Mubarak regime head-on.

9 The Shura Council elections of 2006, municipal council elections in 2007, as well as parliamentary council elections in 2010, saw flagrant violations that in effect barred the election of Brotherhood candidates. See International Crisis Group, 'Egypt's Muslim Brothers: Confrontation or Integration?', Middle East/North Africa Report, no. 76, 18 June 2008, available at http://www.crisisgroup.org/~/media/Files/Middle%20East%20North%20Africa/North%20Africa/Egypt/76_egypts_muslim_brothers_confrontation_or_integration.pdf.

10 'Under the former regime, the state was going to always be hostile to the [Islamic] project and dedicate its vast resources to set it back and combat it. The minimum that needed to be done was to neutralise the state.' Interview

with Brotherhood member and researcher at Ikhwanweb, Cairo, January 2013. It should also be noted that this experience had implications for the movement's internal politics. The more severe the state's repression, the more discredited the reformist wing within the Brotherhood became.

11 Interview with Mohamed Soudan, the FJP head of foreign relations, Alexandria, October 2012.

12 A Brotherhood adviser said that the group wanted a way out of the vicious cycle in which it found itself – the more it practised *daawa*, the more popular it became, and consequently the harder the authorities' response, and therefore the more restricted the movement's ability to practise *daawa*. Interview with a Muslim Brotherhood member and former member of Morsi's staff, Cairo, August 2012. Although many of the group's detractors tend to dismiss its contribution to the uprising, citing its initial reluctance to partake in the 25 January protests, the Brotherhood was indeed at the forefront during the uprising's most decisive days, the 'Friday of Anger' on 28 January and the 'Battle of the Camel' on 3 February. On these two days, the group provided coordinated action and organised mobilisation that ultimately helped bring down the two lethal options at the former regime's disposal: the police force and a network of paid thugs.

13 For a tally of the results, see http://www.elections.eg.

14 'These guys [non-Islamists] are delusional. They think they can cruise into the parliament, but winning takes a lot of hard work, and they do not leave their air-conditioned offices. The *feloul* will crush them. They need our help, but they would not want to let us run on top of the [electoral] lists. Their demands were egregious, which is why we bid them farewell and did our own campaign.' Interview with a Muslim Brotherhood member and senior researcher at Ikhwanweb, Cairo, May 2012.

15 Although Essam al-Erian was in line to become head of the party following Morsi's election, members were told to vote for his rival, Saad al-Katatny, because he was seen as more compliant. Interview with Ibrahim El-Houdaiby, a former Muslim Brotherhood member and senior researcher at the House of Wisdom Foundation for Strategic Studies, Cairo, February 2013.

16 The declaration prompted immense opposition from most other parties, and led to mass demonstrations around the presidential palace. Interview with senior adviser to Khairat al-Shater, January 2013.

17 *Ibid.*

18 The term 'reformist' in this context refers to members of the Brotherhood who advocated the separation of politics from *daawa*, exhorting the group to focus on politics and leave *daawa* to individual initiative. Reformists are often identified as being less confrontational towards outside groups, perhaps adhering more faithfully to Banna's gradualist philosophy. Interview with Abdel Moneim Aboul Fotouh, Cairo, December 2013.

19 At the time, the Brotherhood promised publicly that it would not

nominate a presidential candidate in the forthcoming election.

20 *Tanzimyeen* are those who subscribe to the disciplinary culture that emphasises the movement's hierarchical and secretive spirit. *Tanzimyeen* credit this culture, whose outlook tends to be largely influenced by Nasser's 1960s crackdown, with having preserved the Brotherhood at times of extreme adversity. The reformists, on the other hand, comprise two political generations: the generation of the Brotherhood revival that started in the 1970s, which became active in student and professional unions and in the parliament in the 1980s; and a post-millennial generation of critical younger members, who pushed the movement into insurrection. A group of young urban critics, that was promptly expelled, went on to form the Egyptian Current Party (Al-Tayyar Al-Masri).

21 'The current leadership is unwilling to find a way of realistic, genuine change to rejuvenate the organisation. The Brotherhood was constructed almost like a moulded one-piece car; if the radiator blows up, you cannot replace it, you have to jettison the entire vehicle.' International Crisis Group interview, Ibrahim El-Zaafrani, former senior member of the Muslim Brotherhood, Cairo, September 2012.

22 Hossam Tammam, *The Muslim Brotherhood: The Pre-Revolution Years* (Cairo: Dar al-Shorouk, 2012), pp. 71–136.

23 Within the organisation, the *tanzimyeen* are not perceived as merely a faction, but rather as the legitimate leadership that has helped the Brotherhood survive. To openly go against them is to 'go against legitimacy itself ... the *tanzimyeen* are the Muslim Brotherhood. Vicious repression and the security crackdowns are still a living memory within the group.' Interview with an FJP founding member, Cairo, October 2012.

24 Interviews with Muslim Brotherhood and FJP members, Alexandria, Beni Suef, Cairo, Damietta, Damanhour and al-Mansoura, March–December 2012.

25 These members objected to the group breaking its promises and were wary of the repercussions of what amounted to open confrontation with the interim military government. They preferred a return to the group's historically cautious approach.

26 Interview with an FJP founding member, Cairo, September 2012.

27 After the first round of the presidential election, in which Morsi won about 4% more votes than Ahmad Shafiq, a deputy to the General Guide of the Brotherhood hoped all those who voted for Hamdeen Sabahi and Aboul Fotouh, in third and fourth place respectively, would vote for the 'revolution's candidate', Morsi. Interview with Khairat al-Shater, the deputy to the General Guide, Cairo, May 2012. For complete election results, see 'The Official Site of the Presidential Elections', http://presidential2012.elections.eg/index_results.html.

28 Morsi's slender margin in the second round was met with accusations that military conscripts had voted illegally, and of bribes and voter intimidation. International Crisis Group interviews with Muslim Brotherhood members, Cairo and Alexandria, May–July 2012.

29 Interview with a Muslim Brotherhood member and senior leadership adviser, Cairo, July 2012. Another member, who had initially opposed fielding a candidate, now agreed with the leadership's decision. International Crisis Group interview with the secretary-general of the Brotherhood youth in the Daqahleyya province, al-Mansoura, September 2012.

30 Former Brotherhood member Amr Abu Khalil said: 'They have no desire or time to scrutinise their mistakes and reform themselves. They are being empowered [via elections] as we speak. Why should they?' Interview with Amr Abu Khalil, a former Muslim Brotherhood member, Alexandria, August 2012.

31 The referendum passed with 63.8% of votes, on a comparatively low turnout of 33% of eligible voters. See https://referendum2012.elections. eg/results/referendum-results.

32 Some non-Islamists and technocrats were offered ministerial positions in the second cabinet of Hesham Qandil, but they declined, either because they believed the cabinet was going to be short-lived (forthcoming parliamentary elections), or because they refused to work with an Islamist president. Interview with Muslim Brotherhood member and senior

leadership adviser, Cairo, January 2013.

33 Interview with Muslim Brotherhood member and senior leadership adviser, Cairo, December 2012.

34 Interview with Hisham Gaafar, a former Muslim Brotherhood member and expert on Islamist movements, Cairo, November 2012.

35 Non-Islamists accuse the Brotherhood of adopting a sectarian political strategy. They are grateful for that, however, because they believe the protest movement has expanded its base to include the sizeable Coptic minority. Interview with Shahir Ishaq, founding member of Egypt Freedom Party, Cairo, December 2012.

36 According to a Brotherhood member: 'We saw for the first time the Coptic Church mobilizing massive protests against the Muslim Brotherhood, and the secular opposition was only too happy to receive that kind of support. The Church took a big risk by doing so, and its demands are not revolutionary or progressive at all, but rather factional and sectarian. Its heavy involvement in the situation helped inflame the Islamist anger at the situation.' Interview with Muslim Brotherhood member and senior leadership adviser, Cairo, 31 December 2012.

37 'Egypt: Mass Attacks on Churches', Human Rights Watch, 22 August 2013, http://www. hrw.org/news/2013/08/21/ egypt-mass-attacks-churches.

38 For more information, see International Crisis Group, 'Lost in Transition: The World According to Egypt's SCAF', Middle East/North

Africa Report, no. 12124, Apr 2012, available at http://www.crisisgroup. org/~/media/Files/Middle%20 East%20North%20Africa/North%20 Africa/Egypt/121-lost-in-transition-the-world-according-to-egypts-scaf.pdf.

39 The ruling was unprecedented in how quickly it was adopted, that it did not require a referendum (as with the 1987 parliament whose electoral law was also deemed unconstitutional), and that it was not based on a constitution, because the SCAF had suspended the 1971 constitution after the revolution. Ironically, the SCC's decision may have generated sympathy for the Brotherhood's presidential candidate, Morsi.

40 ElBaradei tweeted that the constitution's supposed contradiction with international law rendered it invalid. See Sahila Hamed, 'El-Baradei: mukhalafit al-dustur fi ba'd mawaduh lil-qanun al-dawly taj'alahu batilan mahma astafta 'alayhu', el-Watan, 26 December 2012, http://www.elwatannews. com/news/details/103653.

41 Interview with Essam El-Haddad, senior foreign-relations adviser to former president Morsi, February 2013.

42 A former non-Islamist adviser of Morsi was sceptical of the chances of success: 'The Brothers' reformist policies towards state institutions and inability to build consensus with other political groups have left them without a choice, but to control all organs of the state. In order to do that, you need to have a charismatic leadership and a robust organisation, and I am not sure they

have either one.' Interview with a former presidential adviser, Cairo, November 2012.

43 Morsi withheld a fact-finding mission's report on the security agencies' involvement and complicity in killings of protesters during the uprising. He also repeatedly praised the leadership of the military and the police force.

44 A member noted most of the jokes about the Brotherhood's 'renaissance project', which promised to improve congested traffic, bread and cooking-gas shortages, and so on, could not be carried out by an uncooperative bureaucracy. As long as the SCAF was breathing down Morsi's neck, and the state seemed to have two heads, the bureaucracy did not worry much about disobeying orders from elected officials. Interview with FJP official, Alexandria, October 2012.

45 Interview with a Muslim Brotherhood member and adviser to senior leadership, Cairo, May 2013.

46 This dynamic became obvious in the appointment of governors, for example, when Morsi initially ignored Brotherhood lobbying to give Hassan el-Brens the governorship of Alexandria. Having realised the inability of the new governor to actively improve services in Egypt's third-largest city, el-Brens was appointed as deputy governor. Interview with Muslim Brotherhood member and senior leadership adviser, Cairo, December 2012.

47 Interview with Amr Adly, then economic programme director at

the Egyptian Initiative for Personal Rights, Cairo, December 2012.

[48] The Brotherhood enjoyed a disproportionate say in shaping the transition in exchange for recognising the SCAF's caretaker administration, as well as suspending protests.

[49] Interview with senior defence-ministry official, Cairo, 8 December 2012.

[50] After explaining that the army would remain part of 'the game' as long as rival factions who 'do not take into account the national interest' continued clashing with one another, a high-ranking general stipulated the conditions under which the military would step in: '1) there has to be popular consensus ...; 2) the goal would be protecting the state itself, and limiting confrontations among political factions; and 3) avoid clashing with the people to secure the integrity of the military'. Interview with a senior defence-ministry official, Cairo, 8 December 2012.

[51] After the 3 July coup, information emerged that leaders of the anti-Morsi group Tamarod, which called for the 30 June protests, were in contact with retired military officers who claimed to speak on behalf of the army's leadership. They promised that the military would protect anti-Morsi protesters. Mike Giglio, 'A Cairo Conspiracy', Daily Beast, 12 July 2013, http://www.thedailybeast.com/articles/2013/07/12/a-cairo-conspiracy.html.

[52] 'When it comes to the army, fear not any coups. As long as General Sisi is minister of defence, be absolutely sure the army will not interfere in politics.' Interview with a member of the presidential staff, Cairo, June 2013.

[53] Matthew Weaver, Paul Owen and Tom McCarthy, 'Egypt Protests: Army Issues 48 Hour Ultimatum', Guardian, 1 July 2013, http://www.theguardian.com/world/middle-east-live/2013/jul/01/egypt-stanoff-millions-protest.

[54] See 'Morsi: the Police Is at the Heart of the 25 January Revolution', https://www.youtube.com/watch?v=TUDQ09SxwcE.

[55] According to a police officer: 'We have been told by our superiors to take a break for the next four years. Let's see how Morsi makes Egyptians feel safe.' Interview with a police officer, Cairo, September, 2012.

[56] Interview with a retired military brigadier, Cairo, November 2012.

[57] 'Egypt: Fresh Assault on Justice', Human Rights Watch, April 2014, http://www.hrw.org/news/2014/04/29/egypt-fresh-assault-justice.

[58] Interviews with senior Brotherhood members, Cairo, August–December 2012.

[59] 'Egypt: Year of Abuses Under al-Sisi', Human Rights Watch, 8 June 2015, https://www.hrw.org/news/2015/06/08/egypt-year-abuses-under-al-sisi.

[60] 'We would want for the moderates and the youths of the organization to eventually denounce their leaders, and that would be the precondition to their reintegration into the political process. The old guard is dead politically, and would receive death sentences very soon.'

Interview with a retired senior security official, Cairo, 7 July 2013. A group called 'Brothers without Violence' formed shortly after the coup, but the Brotherhood's members dismissed it as a creation of the security forces.

61 'The Brotherhood does not entertain the prospect that it could ever lose an election. We are part of the fabric of this society, and we represent its cultural and religious values. It is almost impossible for [a majority of] people to vote for someone else.' Interview with a founding member of the FJP, Cairo, March 2013.

62 Interview with a founding member of the FJP, Cairo, July 2013.

63 Interview with a Muslim Brotherhood member, Cairo, July 2013.

64 'All According to Plan: The Rab'a Massacre and Mass Killings of Protesters in Egypt', Human Rights Watch, August 2014, available at http://www.hrw.org/sites/default/files/reports/egypt0814web.pdf.

65 Interview with a Brotherhood member, January 2014.

66 Khalil El-Anani, 'tahawulat al-hirak al-ikhwani fi misr', al-Arabi al-Jadeed, 2 September 2014, http://www.alaraby.co.uk/opinion/bf1fa467-001f-4bf6-812a-89ebb9e3d5f6.

67 'Masr al-layla: shi'ar rafa'u al-shabab yaqul ma doun al-russas yu'tabar salmiyya', Al Jazeera Mubasher Misr, 29 January 2014, https://www.youtube.com/watch?v=yfLUTPvOj_g.

68 'infirad...7 majmu'at ikhwaniya tubya' da'ish', al-Shorouk, 25 August 2015, http://www.shorouknews.com/news/view.aspx?cdate=25082015&id=be949aa1-769d-4798-9913-336d285e38f2.

69 Al-Jazeera interview with Youssef Nada, former head of foreign relations for the Muslim Brotherhood: 'Bila Hodoud: Neda: inqilab misr sa-yankassir min dakhil al-jaysh', Al-Jazeera Arabic, 17 April 2014, https://www.youtube.com/watch?v=VQV4x00xFKc&index=16&list=PLF80743B97C258B24.

70 Interview with a founding member of the FJP, Cairo, July 2013.

CHAPTER FIVE

Egypt's non-Islamist parties

Michael Wahid Hanna

For many Western observers of the Egyptian uprising, Tahrir Square and the 25 January movement came to be associated with, and defined by, the telegenic faces of the young activists who captured international attention during the uprising's heady early days. This was a function of the disproportionate role these activists played in the early stages of an unexpected mass mobilisation that led to the fall of the regime of long-time dictator Hosni Mubarak, and of the welcome optimism they provided. Perhaps most importantly, though, was the contrast they provided with the Islamist actors who would later come to dominate the post-Mubarak transition. While the seductive narrative of youth activism was overly simplistic, it spoke of a deep hope in the West that the uprisings would lead to inclusive and open governance.

These early impressions and expectations would later colour reactions to the serial political failures of non-Islamist groups. At root, the apparent dominance of Islamist currents in the nascent political order heightened frustration with the performance of the country's non-Islamists.

On one level, this was understandable. More balanced electoral outcomes would provide a more sustainable path for transition. Furthermore, the historical unease with Islamism in the West compounded this sense of disappointment. For years, academics and analysts assumed that more open politics would lead to Islamist political and electoral success. In fact, the prospect of an Islamist takeover was a key defensive mechanism for the Arab authoritarian order – with the implicit message being: it is either us or them. And, of course, the performance of non-Islamist political actors, factions and parties was disastrous in terms of execution and results. Unease over the trajectory of non-Islamist politics and their perceived incompetence pushed Western governments into bolstering support for the Muslim Brotherhood, which appeared to many to have inherited Egyptian politics and established the foundations for prolonged electoral supremacy.

On another level, these assessments about the future of Egyptian and regional politics were based on unfounded assumptions and an ahistorical approach to political transitions, producing analytically faulty conclusions about Egypt's future. Similarly, analysts fell prey to many of these same pitfalls, and most assumed that the Islamists' early success was a harbinger of inevitable future dominance. Egypt and the rest of the region appeared to be on the cusp of a new Islamist era.

Events have confounded those expectations, with Islamists suffering significant losses of support, and avowedly anti-Islamist forces making a show of force in the region. Tragically, for Egypt and beyond, the failures of Islamism have not provided a platform for the forces of reform, inclusion and openness. Instead, the stark binaries that have dominated modern Arab political life persist. Egypt continues to face an arid choice between clashing brands of authoritarianism, with statist nationalism now holding the upper hand over the Brotherhood's version of religious authoritarianism. It is perhaps in the inevitable failure of both of these visions for society that reformist non-Islamist political movements will be resuscitated, but opportunities for this transformation remain a distant prospect.

Defining non-Islamism

In discussing non-Islamist parties, descriptive precision is imperative. Most of the parties comprising this space cannot be described as either secular or liberal. In terms of their approach to sharia and the role of religion in public life, even avowedly secular parties have bowed to the current realities of Egyptian society and ceded the fight over the inclusion of Islamic law. During the transition period, debates over the language of the constitution accepted the existing clauses on sharia as an unalterable starting point for the debate. Calls to preserve the constitution were seen as a defensive step to pre-empt sweeping constitutional changes. At the same time, broad support for the emerging and reinvigorated authoritarian order makes clear the weakness of liberal politics and the limited traction of reformist forces.

The political scene has evolved dramatically since the 2011 uprising. As Khaled Dawoud, official spokesman of al-Dostour Party, has noted, the fall of Mubarak was followed by the establishment of 'dozens of new political parties'[1] that sought to displace 'the old opposition parties that had functioned mainly as a fig leaf for elections that were invariably rigged'.[2] That early phase saw the creation of ostensibly liberal and leftist parties such as the Egyptian Social Democratic Party, the Free Egyptians Party (centre-right), the Socialist Popular Alliance Party, al-Karama Party (a Nasserist offshoot) and a host of smaller parties. Later efforts to consolidate this frag-mented space saw the establishment of al-Dostour, in April 2012, but fragmentation persists, aggravated by the hostility of the regime of President Abdel Fattah Al-Sisi towards open and free politics and independent political-party life. These parties broadly embraced the 25 January uprising and supported the post-Mubarak transition. They later joined forces with other opposition movements to form the National Salvation Front (NSF), a broad-based umbrella group that opposed then-president Muhammad Morsi and the Brotherhood.

Besides the new political parties, revolutionary social groups played a large role in the uprising, as well as the post-uprising protests, although they did not make the full transition into becoming political parties. The most important such group was the 6 April Movement, which organised a number of the anti-Mubarak marches and demonstrations that ultimately led to the 25 January uprising. The movement eventually split into two wings: the Ahmad Maher Front and the Democratic Front. Both opposed the idea of turning 6 April into a political party, preferring to maintain its role as a pressure group that lobbied the government to implement key demands of the 'revolution'. Other groups, such as the avowedly Trotskyite Revolutionary Socialists, were instrumental in organising and sustaining urban protests, but the stridency of their message and their outlier status significantly limited their reach.

The Strong Egypt Party, established by former presidential candidate and Brotherhood member Abdel Moneim Aboul Fotouh, sought to portray itself as a bridge-building endeavour that was economically progressive and socially moderate. While the party was highly critical of the constitutional decree that Morsi issued in November 2012, it did not join the opposition, nor the election boycott. The party never escaped Aboul Fotouh's lifelong association with the Brotherhood, making it difficult to categorise this failed experiment as representative of non-Islamist politics.

Among pre-revolutionary non-Islamist opposition parties, reactions to the uprising was varied. The Nasserist Party, al-Wafd Party and the National Progressive Unionist Party – commonly known as al-Tagammu – were considered to be the three main opposition parties in the pre-uprising era. Although the leaderships of the parties did not associate themselves with the uprising from the beginning, they contested the 2011–12 parliamentary elections. Meanwhile, al-Ghad Party – formed around Ayman Nour, who had unsuccessfully challenged Mubarak in the 2005 presidential election and was later imprisoned on spurious charges – re-emerged in October 2011 under the name of Ghad al-Thawra. However, the party never overcame its personality-driven focus.

A series of parties and factions associated or directly linked with the former regime also emerged. These groups and figures were commonly referred to pejoratively as the *feloul*, meaning 'the remnants of the old regime'. Amid heightened fervour for reform in the months immediately after the fall of Mubarak, supporters of the former regime were largely muted and cautious in their approach to politics. Numerous prosecutions of high-ranking government officials and advisers on corruption charges further restrained their participation. This was most evident during the 2011–12 parliamentary elections, which saw hesitant and disorganised participation by supporters of the former regime. No centralised efforts were made to reactivate the patronage networks of the former ruling National Democratic Party, and the *feloul* parties won only 15 seats in the elections.

The elections had two main non-Islamist components. Al-Wafd briefly aligned itself with the Brotherhood's Freedom and Justice Party (FJP), but after facing outcry from party members it decided to run independently, winning 9.2% of the popular vote, or 41 seats. Two of the new parties, namely the Egyptian Social Democratic Party and the Free Egyptians Party, joined al-Tagammu to form the avowedly anti-Islamist

Egyptian Bloc, which won 31 seats. Businessman Naguib Sawiris financed the Egyptian Bloc almost single-handedly, and his outsized role served to highlight the organisational and financial weaknesses new non-Islamist parties faced. The Revolution Continues Alliance, which comprised activist and leftist groups, won ten seats, while a small number of additional seats were won by various non-Islamist parties. In all, the new parties, in combination with al-Wafd, held approximately 25% of the seats in the new parliament.

The non-Islamist space was overpopulated by redundant political outfits and characterised by a lack of positive vision. Even at the earliest stages of the transition, non-Islamists were essentially defensive, with a view to holding back the rise of political Islam. But mutual distrust between reformists and the *feloul* hampered early efforts to ward off the Islamists' ascendancy, and even tactical efforts were met with outrage by younger cadres and activists. While the leaders of new parties privately conceded the need to eventually join forces with supporters of the former regime, such steps were not possible in practice because of the internal dissent they engendered.[3]

The fraught relationship between reformists and the *feloul* played a major role in fracturing the non-Islamist vote. This conundrum was perfectly demonstrated in the 2012 presidential elections, when non-Islamist rivalry and fragmentation propelled the Brotherhood to an unlikely second-round victory. The terrain of presidential politics in Egypt varied a great deal from the parliamentary setting. While parliamentary elections favour broad-based nationwide political organisations able to nominate candidates who are well known at the district level, presidential politics is far more personality-driven and, as such, less dependent on organisational support. In this sense, the 2012 presidential election was more favourable terrain for the non-Islamist parties. This was clear from the first round, in which the non-Islamist candidates, Ahmad Shafiq, Hamdeen Sabahi and Amr Moussa, collectively garnered over 55% of the vote and finished second, third and fifth respectively. Aboul Fotouh, who came in fourth place, ran a campaign that highlighted his support from both Islamist and non-Islamist figures, positioning himself as a bridge candidate.

The first-round results showed that political allegiances remained fluid, and that non-Islamism could compete and attract votes. Politics was not necessarily an Islamist monopoly, nor was the Brotherhood fated to become a political dynasty. However, the inability to exert discipline before the elections and winnow the field of rival candidates paved the way for the Brotherhood to capture the presidency. After Shafiq, a polarising figure from the old regime, moved on to contest the second round, there was little prospect of victory for the non-Islamist opposition because a significant number of reformists threw their conditional support behind Morsi, in an effort to block the return of the former leadership. Shafiq's campaign marked the wholehearted re-entry of supporters of the former regime into public life, but his ultimate failure was indicative of the abiding divisions that limited the political success of non-Islamist forces.

The broad spectrum covered by non-Islamists (reformists, the *feloul* and youth groups) was a major disadvantage in the presidential election; however, the transitional 18-month period leading up to the election also worked to the Brotherhood's advantage.

Structure and design

The rapid ascent of Egypt's Islamists, led by the Brotherhood, after the fall of the Mubarak regime appeared to validate fundamental assumptions about Egyptian society, religious life and political culture. The initial series of electoral triumphs – in the

March 2011 constitutional referendum, the 2011–12 parliamentary elections and the 2012 presidential election – seemed to vindicate the 'conventional wisdom … that Egyptian citizens display both a desire for God's law and a strong antipathy to nonreligious, leftist ideologies that are thought to have failed around the world', as analyst Tarek Masoud put it.[4] The weakness of non-Islamist parties was the other emerging theme, and became something of a truism in accounts of political life. However, as opposed to being primarily a function of deep-seated societal preferences for Islamism or a reflection of the poor organisational efforts of non-Islamists, this series of disastrous setbacks was much more a reflection of structural legacies and poor transitional design.

The regional rise of Islamism as a counterweight to the long-established Arab authoritarian order accelerated following the crushing defeat of the Egyptian-led Arab armies in the June 1967 war against Israel. Since that watershed moment, political Islam has become a potent regional force, offering a transnational language of dissent. The Arab world and other Muslim-majority societies have witnessed a religious revival that has often expressed itself in the language of renewal and dignity that religious discourse offers. The simple message of political Islam was posited as an antidote to the corrupt, venal and inefficient regimes of the Arab world, and tapped into the sense of humiliation and frustration that typified much of the region. This religious wave also made Islamism a more resilient mode for political dissent and opposition politics in the face of authoritarian repression. The rise of political Islam can also be seen as a reflection of the exhaustion of other alternatives, and the stultified nature of intellectual and political life in the Arab world.

The success of Islamism can be seen in the way in which ostensibly secular authoritarian regimes, such as that in

Egypt, attempted to co-opt Islamic thought and thereby inoculate themselves against criticism on religious grounds. This mainstreaming of Islamist thought left an imprint on Egypt's constitutional, legal, political and social orders and further strengthened the platform for organisations such as the Brotherhood to promote their social and political visions, and to stigmatise secular rivals. As mentioned above, the need to co-opt Islamic principles shaped the debate over a new constitution in the immediate aftermath of Mubarak's fall. In discussions with a broad cross-section of non-Islamist and liberal political leaders and activists, the view was almost unanimous that preserving the existing constitutional formulations over the role of Islam and sharia was a minimum requirement for the country's forthcoming constitution-drafting process.

Furthermore, while Egyptian regimes from that of Gamal Abdel Nasser onwards sought to destroy independent political life and culture, Islamist parties were relatively well prepared to withstand this onslaught. Referring to Nasser's military-led order, Anouar Abdel-Malek argues: 'the officers denied to every other social class, to any national group other than the army, the right and duty to lead the rebirth of Egypt'.[5] Islamist organisation extended beyond the purely political, and made government repression less effective. The organisation of the Brotherhood is all-encompassing for its members, and intrudes on prosaic and quotidian aspects of social interactions and family life. Non-Islamist parties have no such analogues. As Masoud argues:

> [Egypt is] replete with religious institutions, from mosques to religious societies to charitable associations that, though forced to be apolitical during Mubarak's reign, embed both ordinary citizens and Islamist political activists in common networks of

social action, making it easy for the latter to build trust with the former when an opening in the political system finally presented itself.[6]

When Mubarak fell and attention rapidly shifted to canvassing and electioneering, the Brotherhood and other Islamist actors quickly used their organisational advantages to overwhelm nascent non-Islamist rivals. Following the fall of the regime on 11 February 2011, non-Islamist parties had just ten months to overcome these structural advantages – a task that was simply impossible, regardless of commitment and cohesion.

This challenge for non-Islamists was heightened by the initial uncertainty and caution of the *feloul*, who, as mentioned above, did not participate in full force in the early stages of the transition, despite being one of the few non-Islamist groups with existing networks. The Brotherhood therefore encountered a field absent of true peer rivals. With old-regime elements missing from much of the initial contest, the nationwide scope of the Brotherhood's organisational reach and its ability to tap into existing religious networks was further amplified in outlying rural areas, where its advantages were strongest.

The design of the transition itself compounded the disadvantages for non-Islamists in these early stages, because it favoured rapidity and rewarded the largest parties in terms of electoral outcomes. As discussed below, both the Supreme Council of the Armed Forces (SCAF) and the Brotherhood, keen to exploit its organisational advantages, sought a rapid transition. While a slower transition would not have helped non-Islamist parties overcome these challenges, it would have certainly benefited the organisation and party-building process.

As part of the transitional road map, the autumn 2011 parliamentary elections were based on what the International Foundation for Electoral Systems describes as 'a mixed (parallel) system comprised of individual candidate districts (majoritarian two-member, two-round system) and proportional representation lists'.[7] Writing on the eve of the elections, the organisation noted that 'one would expect the new fragmented political reality of Egypt to facilitate seat bonuses for stronger, more experienced political movements', and went on to argue that 'smaller and less entrenched parties could be disadvantaged'.[8] The inclusion of a mixed system, as opposed to one based purely on proportional representation, damaged non-Islamists' prospects and further diluted their representation. They were unable to compete effectively in individual-candidate races, to which national parties with broad operations and notable local personalities are particularly well suited.[9]

From the perspective of electioneering, the Brotherhood's approach was a success,[10] with the FJP winning a dominant position in both houses of the legislature, and ensuring its centrality in the selection of the provisional, 100-member Constituent Assembly tasked with preparing a constitution.

However, the transitional setting and rudimentary nature of party organisation meant that elections were a poor metric for the long-term future of non-Islamists and the trajectory of Egyptian politics. The early transitional elections did not attest to an abiding preference for Islamism as opposed to its alternatives and rivals, including statist nationalism. The crude nature of organisational politics in the non-Islamist sphere and the relatively high levels of voter non-participation meant that electoral results did not fully capture the broad and unarticulated degree of opposition sentiment. At that early juncture of transitional politics, non-Islamist parties remained a poor vehicle for channelling and concentrating diffuse political sentiments, particularly as political allegiances remained remarkably fluid.

As discussed above, the 2012 presidential election sent contradictory signals about electoral preferences, signalling the beginning of shifts that accelerated over the course of Morsi's ill-fated tenure. The collapse of soft, non-ideological support for the Brotherhood during Morsi's presidency was testament to the way in which non-Islamist politics – not to be confused with secularism, reformism or liberalism – can cultivate a significant constituency.

In sum, expectations for rapid non-Islamist electoral success in the post-autocratic environment were naive, as they ignored comparative transitional experiences and the prevailing conditions of that moment in Egyptian history. The self-inflicted wounds of disorganisation, fragmentation and conflicting goals further undermined the electoral performance of non-Islamists, but no amount of industriousness and unity of purpose could have produced the structures necessary to compete in nation-wide parliamentary elections in such a short period of time.

Fracture, dissipation and triangulation

Many of the iconic scenes from Tahrir Square captured the broad array of disparate groups and individuals who joined in protest, to bring down the regime. The success of the uprising was predicated on the fracturing of the regime and state, and the temporary, short-lived solidification of the opposition. This tactical alliance focused primarily on removing the president, and during 18 heady days of protest, it sought to downplay the massive gaps between the different groups and their contradictory visions for the state and society. The military – an institution that retained significant popularity – led in the initial destabilisation of the regime and, ultimately, the removal of the president. This process reversed itself during the Morsi era and in the aftermath of the coup, as the state solidified once again and the opposition fragmented.

The rapid fracturing of the opposition was perhaps the most important development of the post-Mubarak era and was the central factor in shaping relations between the military, Islamists and non-Islamists. It was also the most salient factor in the uprising's failure to bring about consequential systemic reforms. The awkward and short-lived alliance between reformists and mainstream Islamists provided what was perhaps Egypt's only opportunity to jump-start systemic change, but this would have required a degree of trust and convergence that simply did not exist. It would have also required the contending parties and factions to prioritise the establishment of a sustainable, civilian-led political process. Yet the early dynamics of the transition increased the centrality of the military and hastened the collapse of trust among political forces, as electoral politics displaced reform and zero-sum attitudes came to the fore.

With the SCAF firmly in control, the revolution never ruled, and initial fervour for reform was diverted into a procedural transition that was shorn of lasting substantive change. Although the military has come to further dominate political life since the ousting of Morsi and the election of Sisi, this was not an inevitable outcome. In fact, the significant power of opposition solidarity, backed by continual popular protests, was apparent throughout the early stages of transition under the SCAF. In instances in which the broad spectrum of opposition forces remained united, the SCAF was repeatedly forced to retreat and reassess its position. Examples of this can be seen in the ways in which the SCAF dealt with the law governing parliamentary elections, the political-exclusion law and the abolition of the interior ministry's state-security division. However, these instances of opposition unity were exceptional within the general trajectory of the transition: the splits among opposition groups enabled the military to control the political process, and sowed the seeds of mistrust that would plague the rest of the process.

The initial fracturing of the opposition was the result of a convergence of the short-term agendas of the military and the Brotherhood. Immediately after the toppling of Mubarak, the SCAF's fear and misunderstanding of the mass mobilisation led it to seek an implicit pact with the Brotherhood. At that very early stage of the transition, the military clearly believed that the Brotherhood was the only organised political force that it could negotiate with directly, because the organisation had a coherent command-and-control structure able to impose discipline on its cadres. The SCAF generals believed that broad-based popular mobilisation was a by-product of Islamist organisation and discipline,[11] which meant that reaching a tacit understanding with the Brotherhood could bring the protests to a halt. This conclusion was built on the false premise that Islamists were the only political force capable of instigating such mobilisation.

For the Brotherhood, a speedy SCAF-managed transition satisfied its desire for an expedited electoral schedule that would reward its organisational advantages. Deference to the SCAF at that juncture also meant acquiescing to the lack of immediate reforms, precluding transformational politics. The Brotherhood sought to minimise conflict with the SCAF and eschewed direct confrontation with the military, shifting from protest to full-fledged political organisation. With long-awaited electoral success seemingly at hand, the Brotherhood made its own accommodation with power, and limited its criticism of the ruling generals on issues such as the emergency law and military trials for civilians.

With this formative experience in mind, several negative trends began to crystallise. Firstly, reformists came to doubt the potential for cooperative political action with Islamists, as they saw the Brotherhood's behaviour as self-serving and narrowly focused on its own institutional interests, to the detriment of the broader goals that animated the uprising. Secondly, divisions among non-Islamist forces began to emerge over their approach to political change. During the early part of the transition, much of the country remained caught between politics and protest, as many continued to push for further change in line with the unfulfilled demands of the uprising. These protests became a recurring phenomenon, with the reactive SCAF appearing to condition its political programme in accordance with bottom-up pressure. This dynamic reinforced the logic of protests and helped ensure that they continued, while undermining the early efforts of reformist forces to organise politically, as protests and mobilisation still captured their imaginations.

For other non-Islamists, the military began to emerge as the sole counterweight to the ascendant Islamists, and various non-Islamist forces began to assiduously seek their own bargains with the armed forces, particularly as the electoral success of the Brotherhood gathered pace. In the early stages, the pre-existing, discredited opposition parties prioritised the struggle against Islamists, as opposed to the military. An early indication of this approach was the failed effort to draft 'supra-constitutional principles' that would establish core guarantees for rights and liberties, and would mandate the civil nature of the state.

The failure of this effort due to Islamist objections and SCAF manoeuvrings was a harbinger of Egypt's imminent dysfunction; many non-Islamists came to view the military and the state bureaucracy, including the judiciary, as the sole institutional checks against Islamist dominance and religious authoritarianism. While overseeing the transition and triangulating between political forces, the military came to conceive of its role as the guardian of the political process.[12] Many of the SCAF's civilian supporters envisioned the so-called Turkish model – in reference to the Turkish military's one-time dominance of national politics – as a hedge against Islamist rule. While this initial effort receded temporarily, it laid the foundation for mutual distrust between the SCAF and Islamist parties.

Brotherhood maximalism

The behaviour of non-Islamist actors was heavily influenced throughout the transition by the maximalist behaviour of the Brotherhood, particularly as the politically successful alliance between the Brotherhood and the Salafists appeared to provide the former with a route to consolidating its rule and co-opting the organs of the state. While the Brotherhood saw the nascent Salafist parties as its main political rivals, the two factions aligned on a variety of issues in opposition to non-Islamists, particularly with regard to the structure of the transition and the drafting of the constitution. As opposed to pushing the Brotherhood to moderate its position, the unexpected electoral success of the Salafists fostered greater emphasis on Islamist credentials. This intra-Islamist comity would later collapse, as the Brotherhood's erstwhile Salafist allies came to deplore the movement's penchant for unilateralism and zero-sum politics.

The Brotherhood's maximalism, coupled with its incompetent governance, fuelled the massive backlash that produced the 30 June protests and Morsi's overthrow. This backlash was broad-based, and temporarily brought together forces across the non-Islamist spectrum and diluted Salafist support for Morsi and the Brotherhood.

The series of electoral successes experienced by the Brotherhood, beginning with the March 2011 referendum, reinforced the movement's pre-existing perceptions of its role in society and politics, and the nature of its mandate. The Brotherhood saw the series of elections held throughout 2011 and 2012, which in many ways represented the final elections of the Mubarak era, as reflecting an essential aspect of the political and religious preferences of Egyptians. But the structural impediments affecting non-Islamist parties and the rudimentary nature of their organisational efforts suggested that these early electoral results were a poor indicator of future performance. This could be seen in the way that soft, non-ideological support for the Brotherhood collapsed during Morsi's ill-fated tenure.

From the perspective of the reformists, the Brotherhood's initial decision to pursue a formalistic procedural transition that eschewed substantive reform instilled doubts and damaged trust. This was compounded by the Brotherhood's attempt to rapidly stigmatise opposition and dissent. Despite this breakdown of trust, many activists and reformists nonetheless threw their support behind Morsi during the run-off presidential election to pre-empt the return of the old regime in the figure of Shafiq. This support was predicated on a series of concessions on a more inclusive approach to governance that had been agreed with the Brotherhood. Crucially, the Brotherhood agreed to appoint a diverse, broad-based and representative Constituent Assembly, which would be tasked with drafting a new constitution.

Once in power, the Brotherhood wholly ignored these agreements. Furthermore, it sought to disable the remaining, limited checks and balances, with Morsi focusing attention on neutering the judiciary. As with other institutions of the state, the judiciary was in desperate need of reform. However, based on the Brotherhood's approach to governance, non-Islamists could only interpret efforts at unilateral reform as an attempt to capture state institutions, rather than measures undertaken in good faith.

While the Brotherhood's ability to strengthen its hold on the bureaucracy was largely aspirational at this stage, the runaway fears of non-Islamists were reinforced by the disastrous constitutional declaration of November 2012, which set Egypt on course for an inevitable confrontation. The declaration itself sought to temporarily insulate Morsi and his decisions from judicial oversight, with the aim of clearing the obstacles to the adoption of a new Brotherhood-led constitution. This fateful step engendered broad-based opposition from groups that included segments of the urban poor and various rural constituencies, and eventually culminated in the 30 June protests.

The Brotherhood, however, was intoxicated by its success, and saw the declaration as an opportunity to consolidate its grip on power. This initial success also bred a sense of superiority with respect to non-Islamist opponents, whom the movement viewed as weak elitists who were out of step with the true desires of Egyptians. The Brotherhood's overconfidence blinded it to the ways in which its popularity was being eroded. In this sense, the scale of the 30 June protests and the reaction of the armed forces came as a shock to Morsi and the Brotherhood.

The fears of the Brotherhood's opponents surpassed the reality on the ground, but with no obvious near-term checks on the movement's power, its opponents feared the worst, often excessively so. The Brotherhood's control of the state and the bureaucracy was much more tenuous than appearances suggested. However, during this foundational moment, when the opportunity arose to reorder Egypt's constitutional and political framework, inclusivity was a necessary ingredient for stability. Lacking this, the imbalances raised the stakes and undermined efforts at compromise. They also bred a penchant for non-cooperation and an enthusiasm for boycotts among many non-Islamists, who began to search for other checks on the power of the Brotherhood and its allies.

The political crisis over the constitutional declaration and the constitution-drafting process pushed non-Islamist political forces together and hastened the formation of the NSF. However, this umbrella group was only representative of a shared distrust of the Brotherhood. The group's efforts were hobbled by the enduring division in the non-Islamist bloc between reformists and the *feloul*.

Tensions were heightened by defining structural imbalance in the Constituent Assembly and the enormity of the stakes involved. The imbalance also diverted attention away from the process of party-building and grassroots organisational efforts. Boycotts became the favoured tactic, and they were carried out in an effort to weaken the moral legitimacy of the transition. This high-risk approach was successful in stigmatising the constitution-drafting process and the resulting document, despite its subsequent ratification by popular referendum. However, renewed threats to boycott upcoming parliamentary elections divided the non-Islamist camp.

In spring 2013, with a new constitutional order and the organisational advantages of the Brotherhood and its allies still in place, the prospects for non-Islamists appeared bleak. However, the continuing incompetence and arrogance of the Brotherhood offered the non-Islamist camp a reprieve, and the serial blunders of Morsi furthered the military's loss of confidence in the ability of the organisation to provide much-needed stability.

Non-Islamist efforts still relied on the well-rehearsed tactic of organised protest, which had again come to replace any sense of strategic vision. The scope of the anti-Morsi backlash and the building sense of opportunity unified the non-Islamist sphere and mobilised previously quiescent sectors of the public, resulting in an unprecedented mobilisation against Morsi's presidency. Among the participants in the 30 June protests, there were differing views as to desired outcomes, with some demonstrators explicitly working for a military intervention and others seeking concessions or the resignation of Morsi. It is clear that all participants were unprepared for the scope and size of the protests, which changed the calculations of the opposition and, fatefully, of the military.

The death of possibility

During the protests, the fragmented non-Islamist groupings momentarily became a unified political force. The spectre of the Brotherhood consolidating its rule was enough for them to briefly overcome the central divide that had typified non-Islamist politics; namely, their views on the 25 January uprising. This convergence has collapsed as the new military regime, led by Sisi, has intently focused on consolidating its grip on power and reaffirming the centrality of the state. There is now little room for tolerating, let alone nurturing, independent political forces and parties.

The coherence of the non-Islamist sphere during the 30 June protests began to fracture due to differing views of the military coup that removed Morsi from office. This fault line represented varying aspirations for the protests. There were several possibilities – Morsi's resignation, scheduling early elections or holding a national referendum on allowing him to remain in office – that would have had near unanimous support within the non-Islamist sphere, but even at this early stage there were also some individuals who opposed military intervention. However, dissenting views among non-Islamists, such as those espoused by noted liberal Amr Hamzawy,[13] were in a distinct minority in the immediate aftermath of the coup. The vast majority of reformists supported the military's intervention, despite the fact that it was wholeheartedly backed by supporters of the former regime. Principles were sidelined – especially after the outbreak of the protests, when it became clear that Morsi had in effect lost control of the state and the bureaucracy, and was president in name only.

At this juncture, the path forward hinged on the decision-making and judgement of the military. Due to their unhappy experience during the SCAF's stewardship, some reformists saw the coup less as a power grab by the military than as an opportunity to begin a more sustainable and equitable transition process. Prominent figures from the Egyptian Social Democratic Party took positions in the first post-Morsi cabinet, including the premiership, and noted opposition figure Mohamed ElBaradei assumed the position of interim vice-president.

The direction of the military-led political order began to emerge shortly thereafter, as the security establishment was given broad licence to deal with the Islamist-led opposition to the coup. ElBaradei and a small group of reform advocates within the government sought a political settlement to the gathering crisis with the Brotherhood, in the face of 'eradicationist' sentiment from hardline elements of the security establishment.[14] Regional and international diplomatic efforts sought to support these ultimately fruitless negotiations.

More serious strains on this broad support appeared after the brutal and violent dispersal of pro-Morsi protesters at Rabaa al-Adawiya and al-Nahda squares on 14 August. Those advocating a political settlement with the Brotherhood, such as ElBaradei, believed that hardliners had ultimately sabotaged the negotiations, and that their efforts had not been dealt with in good faith. Following the breakdown of the talks, the crisis escalated and ultimately led to the violent and unprecedented crackdown. This resulted in the deaths of at least 817 people.[15] It also led to the resignation of ElBaradei and the first major fissure among the reformist forces. However, support for the interim military-led political order remained robust, and El Baradei's departure did not inspire other resignations.

Those initial strains would grow more pronounced over time, as the military tightened its hold on political life. Nevertheless, due to emerging security threats, broad-based regime support and the absence of immediate political alternatives, doubts and disagreements did not produce significant opposition. This caution was further reinforced by both the sense of existential struggle and the ferocity of regime repression. In Egypt's post-coup environment, dissent was seen as tantamount to treason. Following his resignation, ElBaradei was subject to a state-orchestrated campaign of character assassination and legal threats, prompting him to flee the country.

As the military-led transition continued, it became clear that the security establishment was comprehensively reasserting its control and a resurgent statism emerged as the ordering principle of political life. The ways in which Sisi and the regime relate to political parties will be a critical factor in Egypt's future. Based on his presidential campaign and short tenure in office, it appears that Sisi would like to be seen as the protector of the state and system, yet above the prosaic politics of party life. During his campaign, his advisers largely eschewed the more rudimentary aspects of political mobilisation that had been embraced and cultivated by the Shafiq campaign. This choice helped depress overall voter turnout. More importantly, the indifferent approach to the parliamentary elections, and the flawed legal framework governing them, indicates a hostile attitude towards independent political-party life.

At this juncture, even steadfast supporters of Sisi have become concerned over the opacity of decision-making and the monopolistic impulses of a rejuvenated security establishment. These concerns have remained largely private, because the non-Islamist parties have adopted a defensive approach, seeking to carve out some space for independent political activity that is separate from the machinations of the regime. There are such doubts even within some of the parties most closely connected to the former regime.[16] Complaints have centred on the proposed structure of parliamentary elections and the privileging of single-member districts over a party-list system, which would be likely to cripple the nascent non-Islamist political sphere. Within this inauspicious setting, reformists 'feel ignored by a popular president, attacked relentlessly by the media, and have no tradition of multiparty activity to draw from',[17] as Dawoud has said. More recently, criticisms have become more commonplace, and have been aired publicly as the elections were repeatedly delayed.

The Sisi regime is in a strong position, with much of Egyptian society exhausted by the tumult of recent years, fearful of rising domestic terrorism and violence, as well as regional instability, lacking genuine political alternatives, and continuing to support the military. During this reactionary phase, Egypt is unlikely to witness major course corrections or political openings, and is equally unlikely to achieve significant and sustainable economic, security or political progress.

As the regime has continued to consolidate its power while re-energising the hierarchies within the state, it has sought to funnel political activity towards support for the government, to the detriment of political groups. It has also shown zero tolerance for dissent and has at best stigmatised – and at worst criminalised – the 25 January uprising itself. Members of youth groups such as 6 April, which have actively called for a third way beyond the dichotomy between the military and Islamists, have faced arbitrary detentions, trials in military courts and prison sentences. While this outcome was not self-evident on 3 July 2013, it is unmistakable that an authoritarian relapse has taken root and defined the country's current political course. As this consolidation has taken place, the organs of the state have closed ranks around a common agenda, despite continuing internal rivalries. Notwithstanding such internal differences, the institutions of the state have for the most part remained outwardly united, and have prevented tactical disagreements and competition from muddling the public discourse.

Alongside this statist project, the non-Islamist sphere itself has remained fractured, with persistent divisions among reformists, and a serious and unbridgeable divide between some reformists and supporters of the former regime. The re-emergence of state-centric politics and prevailing hyper-nationalism are indicative of the weak social base of the reformist and secular parties.

Perhaps most consequentially, the irreparable breach of trust between reformists and mainstream Islamists means that the alignment of forces that brought about the 25 January uprising will not be recreated, ensuring that the state and regime have no near- to medium-term peer rivals. Egypt's trajectory remains troubled, and the Sisi regime shows no sign of having recognised the true nature of the country's interlinked political, security and economic crises. For non-Islamists, the inevitable failures of the current regime, and the recent failures of the Islamist movement, will eventually provide an opportunity to again construct viable political alternatives for the country. For Egypt, and the Arab world more broadly, it remains unclear whether non-Islamists are up to this monumental long-term challenge.

Notes

1   Khaled Dawoud, 'Secular Parties in Egypt's Political Landscape', Middle East Institute, 11 September 2014, http://www.mei.edu/content/secular-parties-egypts-political-landscape.

2   *Ibid.*

3   Interview with senior political-party official, November 2011.

4   Tarek Masoud, *Counting Islam: Religion, Class, and Elections in Egypt* (New York: Cambridge University Press, 2014), p. xiii.

5   Anouar Abdel Malek, *Egypt:*

Military Society: The Army Regime, the Left, and Social Change under Nasser (New York: Random House, 1968), p. 178.

6   Masoud, *Counting Islam*, p. 6.

7   International Foundation for Electoral Systems, 'Elections in Egypt: Analysis of the 2011 Parliamentary Electoral System', November 2011, p. 3, http://www. ifes.org/~/media/Files/Publications/ White%20PaperReport/2011/ Analysis_of_Egypts_2011_ Parliamentary_Electoral_System. pdf.

8   *Ibid.*, p. 4.

9   This experience is in contrast with events in Tunisia where, paradoxically, a fortuitous election design, coupled with the dominant position of the Islamist an-Nahda party, played a major role in producing a balanced and sustainable political process. Tunisia's October 2011 elections for the country's first Constituent Assembly were based on a closed-list proportional-representation system. See John M. Carey, 'Electoral Formula and the Tunisian Constituent Assembly', working paper, May 2013, http:// sites.dartmouth.edu/jcarey/ files/2013/02/Tunisia-Electoral-Formula-Carey-May-2013-reduced. pdf. In fact, while an-Nahda received approximately 38% of the vote, no other party list received even 10% of the vote. In effect, the party 'paid "full price" (quota) for most of its seats while everyone else got theirs almost exclusively wholesale (by remainders)', as John Carey put it. Private Correspondence. In Egypt, in contrast, the more evenly distributed vote share meant that the distortions between vote share and seat share on the proportional-representation side of the elections were minimal, despite the fact that the country also employed a Hare quota with the largest remainders.

10 The FJP won 216 seats or 43.4% of the lower house of parliament, and the ultraconservative Salafist Nour Party and its hardline Islamist allies won 125 seats, or 25%. The lower house was designed to be the dominant house of parliament in the selection process, in contrast to the historically more perfunctory role of the upper house.

11 Interview with a senior SCAF adviser, Cairo, August 2011.

12 During early discussions, SCAF sympathisers raised the idea of giving the military the explicit authority to protect Egypt's constitutional order and civil state.

13 Additionally, Aboul Fotouh's Strong Egypt Party took a similar line in the 30 June protests; it took part but opposed direct military intervention to remove Morsi from office.

14 Interview with a former senior Egyptian government official, Cairo, March 2014.

15 Human Rights Watch, 'All According to Plan: The Rab'a Massacre and Mass Killings of Protesters in Egypt', August 2014, p. 6, available at http://www.hrw. org/sites/default/files/reports/ egypt0814web.pdf.

16 Private correspondence with a senior political-party official.

17 Dawoud, 'Secular Parties in Egypt's Political Landscape', p. 3.

CHAPTER SIX

Civil society

Dr H.A. Hellyer

Prior to the 2011 uprising, there was considerable scepticism about the state of Egypt's civil society and therefore the wisdom of any disruption of its political system. Civil society was viewed as lethargic at best, or even nearly extinct, following its repression under the regime of Hosni Mubarak. Consequently, a revolution was seen as potentially exposing this gaping hole, causing instability and costing Egyptian society dearly.

Despite tremendous restrictions, a semblance of civil society persisted. The Mubarak regime occasionally allowed certain openings: some Islamist movements, such as the Muslim Brotherhood and Salafi groups, found room to operate – but mostly in domains that were not directly or overtly political. This partially explains the social capital that such groups had after 2011, which they translated into political capital. In general, though, it was believed that civil society could not countenance, let alone manage, the political and social aftershocks of radical change.

What followed the events of January 2011 both contradicted and validated such scepticism. Wholly unexpectedly, civil society rose to the challenge during the 18 days of the uprising.

Groups and networks of activists had survived, despite having been pushed to the margins, and they managed to organise, showing skill and commitment. Others arose, instinctively and intuitively, as organic groupings such as neighbour-hood-watch committees, which emerged to fill security gaps that were created when the police withdrew from the streets. Together, they managed to sustain the country until Mubarak was removed from power, and the uprising 'ended'.

Four years on, it is deeply questionable whether the uprising achieved its aims – the consensus point was the removal of Mubarak, but little beyond that. Other chapters in this book tackle some of the ways that the uprising affected, or did not affect, the workings of the state and society. One aspect that remains under-examined, however, is how civil society in particular evolved during the four turbulent years that followed the ouster of Mubarak. This chapter traces the transformation of four civil-society clusters since 2011: youth, non-governmental organisations (NGOs), labour movements and the media.

Civil society, particularly civil-rights organisations, played a significant role in the immediate post-uprising period. Nonetheless, such groups were progressively marginalised, with the exception of political groupings, such as the Brotherhood or Salafi groups, before the 2013 coup. The curtailment of the 2011 democratic experiment by the coup subjected civil society to even more legal restrictions. It is now more fragmented than before – but it has also learned key lessons from the 2011–13 period, and has matured in certain ways. It remains to be seen how those lessons can be leveraged in the future.

Youth

The demographics of Egypt played a direct role in fostering the conditions that led to the 2011 uprising. The markedly large percentage of young people relative to the rest of the population and a lack of economic opportunity fed a sense of exclusion and political disenfranchisement. Around 60% of the population is considered to be 'youth', with around one-third between the ages of 10 and 24. The average age of an Egyptian in 2015 was about 24 years old – and that average is falling. The official unemployment rate among Egyptians was around 13.4%,[1] and according to national statistics for 2013, more than half of the unemployed population was aged 15–24. An additional 23% of those who were unemployed were from the 25–29 age bracket,[2] a fact that underscores lack of work as a critical challenge for young people in Egypt.

The decision by activist youth movements to resort to street action in 2011 was the culmination of years of preparation, as well as frustration with mainstream opposition parties. Among them were groups such as 6 April, which was born out of labour strikes in Mahalla al-Kubra in 2008 and dominated by non-ideological youth sympathetic to certain liberal and leftist ideas. It was neither a secularist movement nor an Islamist one, which made it flexible in terms of its membership.

While protests in January and February 2011 represented society at large, young people played a disproportionately large role in them. Contrary to media reports on the role of social media as the chief platform for mobilisation, only a few of the protesters actually used social media.[3] Youth movements played a central part in all aspects of the uprising, from enrolling in established political parties to leading street action. This included the establishment of the 'Revolutionary Youth Coalition', which formed in Tahrir Square during the 18 days of uprising, and other political coalitions such as 'Revolution Continues'. Notably, younger members of more established groups, such as the Muslim Brotherhood, broke away from their parent bodies – or were forced out – because they participated in independent, revolutionary politics.

Relying on street mobilisation even after Mubarak's resignation, the youth became key actors in the dynamic civil society that emerged in 2011. For a while, youth organisations posing as the guardians of revolutionary principles shaped the public agenda and became a significant pressure group that the military and the political parties had to engage with and placate. Young people engaged in protests and marches on a variety of issues and launched extensive campaigns, including 'No to Military Trials for Civilians' and 'Military Liars' (later also 'Brotherhood Liars'). Even though much youth activity was ad hoc, some revolutionary youth joined political parties: they were instrumental, for example, in the founding of the Egyptian Social Democratic Party, and they had significant representation in the Constitution Party, but they were not offered leadership roles.

In the 2012 presidential election, young people were as divided as the country was – those favouring the revolution appeared to back more explicitly pro-revolutionary candidates, such as Abdel Moneim Aboul Fotouh, a liberal-leaning former Brotherhood leader, and Hamdeen Sabahi, a leftist/Nasserist candidate. Others voted for lesser-known leftist and revolutionary candidates such as Khaled Ali. The second round – a choice between Ahmed Shafiq, a Mubarak-era military figure, and Muhammad Morsi of the Brotherhood – placed voters in a quandary. Would the revolution be served better by abstaining altogether? Would Morsi, a right-wing, reactionary Islamist leader who nonetheless did not belong to the security state, be better than Shafiq, who clearly represented the former regime? Despite the intensity of the debate, it is difficult even now to establish how the revolutionary-youth vote eventually split.

Young people were also broadly present in the mass protests against Morsi in late June and early July 2013. Many among the revolutionary youth backed the Tamarod (Rebel) movement in calling for an early presidential election – as did nearly all of the non-Islamist political forces in the country. Indeed, even some of the Islamist-leaning politicians, such as Aboul Fotouh, backed the call for early presidential elections and joined the 30 June protests. A split occurred over the coup on 3 July, which created a new set of challenges for youth movements. Some of the youth had already gone home by then, as it became clear that the military was taking a prominent role in 'fulfilling' Tamarod's requests.

While many Egyptians backed the coup, the revolutionary youth were profoundly divided. Some were willing to give the military a chance, presuming it had 'learnt its lesson' after 2011. Others were more sceptical: military involvement in politics mis-served both the country and the army. A 'third way' – neither Muslim Brotherhood nor military – was advocated by smaller revolutionary organisations, such as a group that became known as the 'Third Square'. While such dissent and opposition remain, the military has designed a new environment that has restricted youth groups from organising and mobilising, and that has confined anyone who challenges the new political order to the margins.

The state has cracked down heavily on demonstrations. A restrictive protest law, passed in November 2013, removed one of the main legal avenues for dissent. It imposes hefty jail sentences on those who participate in unauthorised demonstrations.[4] Most demonstrations held since the army retook power have been in support of the now-banned Brotherhood, calling for the reinstatement of Morsi, but a substantial number have been organised for other causes as well.

Hundreds of young protesters have been imprisoned under the November 2013 law, and several human-rights organisations say the number of political prisoners has risen above 41,000. This includes supporters of Morsi, but also non-Islamist critics of the government of Abdel Fattah Al-Sisi, such as Alaa Abdel Fattah, Sana Seif and Ahmed Maher. All three have a substantial following among revolutionary youth: Maher is a prominent 6 April leader, and Sana Seif is a young activist from the same well-known family of activists as Alaa Abdel Fattah, himself a key independent revolutionary activist. The effect of this on the youth's political consciousness should not be underestimated.[5]

Unverified reports indicate that 'official' modes of political mobilisation that the state favours, such as the constitutional referendum of early 2014 or the presidential election later that year, did not attract the youth in large numbers. NGOs claimed that such polls relied more on elderly voters than the young, which had not been the case in previous electoral exercises.[6]

The government also seemed attuned to this: its decision to arrange meetings with young activists showed concern over the issue of youth disenfranchisement from the political process. Former interim president Adly Mansour held three dialogue sessions with youth representatives in December 2013 and January 2014, and the interior minister had hosted a similar meeting earlier, but as noted by Egyptian journalist Mostafa Hashem, neither seemed to allay youth groups' concerns about

> the protest law, the use of violence against demon-
> strators, the arrest of hundreds of activists, the state
> media's negative portrayals of the January 25 revolu-
> tion, the leaking of activists' wiretapped phone calls
> on a satellite channel, and the return of prominent
> Mubarak-era leaders into the government.[7]

In 2015 it did not appear that the latest political dispensation in Cairo had fully appreciated the potential repercussions of not engaging young people more fully in mainstream political life. A substantial proportion of young people showed signs of despair – and severe limitations on the peaceful expression of dissent through protests have given rise to more violent methods. In some demonstrations, young Egyptians have destroyed police property, infuriated by lack of reform in the security sector. Youth-dominated, intensely pro-football groups ('Ultras') have clashed with the police on several occasions, often resulting in the deaths of young people due to excessive police force.

Already, a significant number of Morsi supporters are suspected to have turned away from peaceful protest, and young people in particular have called for violence. As one reporter notes:

> At a recent pro-Brotherhood demonstration, a young man could be seen holding a sign that said, 'Peacefulness has killed us', going on to criticise the Brotherhood-backed group that had organised the demonstrations for insisting on nonviolence even in the face of police gunfire.[8]

The failure to properly engage with young people in Egypt, particularly at a time when youth unemployment is at a critical state, is likely to have serious repercussions. Given the country's current malaise and the deterioration of key political, social and economic indicators, analysts and commentators suspect that youth who joined the 2011 uprising may mobilise once more. This is not entirely clear, but many of the networks that developed since 2011 continue to operate, albeit on the periphery. Should a sizeable proportion of young people continue to feel marginalised and excluded, finding no effective means of expressing dissent through official channels, they may coalesce and mobilise in a destructive manner. If they do, the Egyptian state will be both a target and a cause of such discontent.

NGOs

NGOs operate at the nexus of civil society, the security state and the international community. They come in a variety of forms: associations, foundations, non-profit companies, law firms and unions. Civil-society groups often seek legal recognition by registering as NGOs, and then find themselves subjected to restrictive regimes.

Several infamous laws passed in 2002 by the Mubarak regime have governed NGOs: the Law on Associations and Community Foundations[9] and the Ministry of Social Solidarity's Implementing Regulation for Law 84.[10] According to these laws, NGOS must officially register with the government, while grounds for denial of registration are unclear. NGOs are forbidden from engaging in 'political activities', and the ministry is required to approve any affiliation with a foreign entity, whether it receives funding or not. Although widespread NGO and international opposition has prevented the enforcement of these laws, they have been invoked to harass groups. As others have pointed out,[11] the goal of these laws is not to eliminate NGOs, but to provide the government with discretionary powers – meaning that it can change the 'rules of the game' when it chooses to do so.

Since 2011, those 'rules' have become increasingly – many would say, deliberately – vague. Since Mubarak's ouster, successive administrations have tried to establish a legal regime for NGOs, but often within the framework of the 2002 laws.[12] Each time, human- and civil-rights organisations have expressed concerns that the suggested legislation will simply restrict NGOs' freedom rather than regulate them in a fair manner. Every time a government has tried to move against NGOs, these organisations have drawn attention to Egypt's international legal commitments, and the international community has often sided with them: for example, the subject of NGOs and the reduction of the public space in which they operate was raised many times at the United Nations Universal Periodic Review (UPR) in 2014.[13]

Pleas from international bodies on behalf of NGOs have always been a sensitive subject for the state. The security establishment is deeply suspicious of their work, especially in the field of human rights, and of their links to foreign entities – long perceived as a potential threat to the state's sovereignty. Indeed, European and North American governments and foundations are prime financial supporters of these organisations, and the security services often assume that the NGOs do their bidding.

The June 2013 'foreign funding' case illustrates these tensions. It resulted in the imprisonment of 43 local and foreign staff from five international NGOs, who were given sentences of between one and five years. Their infringements of local legal codes included 'managing unlicensed branches' of their organisations, 'conducting research, political training, surveys, and workshops without licenses', 'training political parties and groups' and 'illegally receiving foreign funding'.[14] The foreign organisations included branches of Freedom House, the International Republican Institute, the National Democratic Institute, the International Center for Journalists and the Konrad Adenauer Foundation. This case was split in two: the first part of it related to international NGOs, and the second to local organisations that had received foreign funding.

The case reflected a resurgence of the security apparatus and old-regime stalwarts, including those within the judiciary. The message seemed to be that, as the guardians of the state, they would not allow such civil-society activity to take place, except on their terms. The impact of this message on NGOs that received foreign funding, whether Egyptian ones or branches of international ones, was immediate and chilling.

This case also indicates the unchanged stance towards NGOs each of the post-revolutionary administrations has adopted: the aid workers involved in it were first arrested in 2012 under the Supreme Council of the Armed Forces; the verdict came out in June 2013 under Morsi (the Brotherhood authorities acquiesced to the case in an attempt to co-opt parts of the establishment) and was upheld after his removal in July. The situation since has not improved – if anything, it has deteriorated.

The constitution passed in 2014 contains a number of provisions that, if fully applied, would allow NGOs to operate more freely. However, the clause 'as determined by law' allows the state to limit in practice constitutional freedoms that exist in theory. A new ultimatum issued after Sisi became president further affected the legal framework for NGOs: they were ordered to register under Mubarak's 2002 NGO law while a new NGO law was being drafted. Many organisations were concerned that that to register under the old law, with the legal regime it entailed, would in effect end their independence. Registration under the 2002 law places excessive restrictions on funding, interferes with the independence of these groups[15] and eases the application of harsh penalties for infringements.

In response to the ultimatum, 45 national and international NGOs issued a joint statement, refusing to register by the 2 September deadline.[16] While some have held their ground and continue their activities while unregistered, others have registered: according to official figures for 2014, 89 foreign NGOs were registered and authorised to work in Egypt, in addition to some 40,000 registered Egyptian organisations.[17] The decision to register was most likely an attempt to prevent conflict with the state, as the authorities indicated that unregistered NGOs would be pursued one way or another.

The regime's attitude toward NGOs mirrors its approach to other components of civil society. The government often sees

NGO criticism as unwarranted, inherently hostile or politically charged, and blames it for weakening the country's morale, institutions and cohesion. Amnesty International notes that the 'Egyptian authorities are sowing a climate of fear which has stopped NGOs from doing their vital work of defending human rights and the law'. For example, a group of NGOs refused to participate, as would have been normal, in the UPR, citing fears of retribution in Egypt.

International advocacy group Human Rights Watch (HRW) consistently criticised human-rights violations committed by the Morsi government, but its criticism of the Sisi regime has earned it new-found disdain among large parts of Egypt's media and officialdom. An HRW delegation was denied entry to Egypt in August 2014, as it planned to publicise an investigative report on the killing of around 1,000 civilians when the authorities broke up a pro-Morsi sit-in at Rabaa al-Adawiya and al-Nahda squares. Tellingly, Egypt's quasi-official human-rights organisation, the National Council for Human Rights, has launched a court case against HRW in Egypt.

This comes against the backdrop of a 'war on terror' that shapes policy and a media that generally frames dissent of any kind as treasonous. The presidency decreed new counter-terrorism legislation in February 2015, which has targeted civil society – including NGOs – for what were hitherto legitimate activities. Article 1 of the new law broadly defines 'terrorist entities' to include 'any association, organisation, group or gang' that attempts to:

> destabilise the public order; endanger the wellbeing or safety of society … endanger social unity … obstruct the work of public authorities, the judiciary, government entities, or local municipalities … block public or private transportation, or roads; harm national unity

or threaten national peace; or obstruct the implementation of the constitution or laws or bylaws.[18]

Such a wide definition of terrorism could well affect NGOs
engaged in research and advocacy. While the state has always
been hostile towards NGOs, these new laws amount to a
qualitative escalation at a critical juncture. Many NGOs that
work on civil and human rights play a key role in verifying
facts at a time when neutral observers view both pro-state
and pro-Brotherhood media with suspicion, and when state
institutions, including the judiciary, are seen as unreliable
and adversarial.

One might have hoped that, after the upheavals of the past
few years, the state would have realised that grassroots organisations and civil-rights groups do not generally threaten
society, but rather strengthen it. If given the opportunity to
carry out their work without interference, they will, in the
short, medium and long term, assist in improving society as
a whole. Any fulfilment of the aims of the 2011 uprising is
rather difficult to envision without strengthening the independence and the space provided to NGOs. At the moment,
it is not only their independence that is at risk for many, but
their very existence.

Labour

An underappreciated player in Egypt's civil society is the
labour movement. The sole legal trade-union body is the
Egyptian Trade Union Federation (ETUF), which was officially
registered in 1976. Since its inception, the ETUF has essentially
been an instrument of the state. Its members work primarily in
the public sector, which accounts for around 60% of the official economy. The sector is composed of companies that are
under the direct control of the government, its ministries or the

military establishment, which owns many manufacturing and construction firms.[19]

Nevertheless, the ETUF was unable to stop the numerous strikes that took place over the two decades before the 2011 uprising. According to some estimates, some 4,000 strikes involving as many as four million participants were held.[20] The main grievances flowed from opposition to economic-liberalisation policies that started in 1974, under Anwar Sadat, and accelerated under Mubarak. Dissatisfaction with the liberal policies of the government of Prime Minister Ahmed Nazif led to widespread and continuous mobilisation in 2004, which fed into a broader tide of discontent. Labour strikes at a textile plant in Mahalla al-Kubra in April 2008, which at the time went largely unreported, were motivated by underlying socio-economic grievances that would fuel the 2011 uprising. The strikes shaped the mindset and organisation of youth activists: the prominent 6 April movement took its name from the date of the Mahalla al-Kubra strike.

The situation in the labour sector has deteriorated under the Sisi government. Strikes and protests are illegal and independent civil action is often construed as an attack on the state, which makes it difficult for the labour movement to operate. No steps have been taken to reverse this; on the contrary, the former minister of manpower, Nahed al-Ashry, and his successor both opposed strikes.[21] A number of laws instituted by the presidency since July 2013, including the Civil Services Law, the Investment Law and the Unified Labour Law, serve to stifle the labour sector.[22] Labour movements and syndicates harshly criticise the centralisation of recruitment that results from these laws, as do groups such as the Revolutionary Socialists, which agitates for workers' rights. Furthermore, independent, non-state-affiliated labour unions continue to be unrecognised due to a legal obstacle dating from 1976.

The government is considering further legislation, including a ban on sit-ins at the workplace. Civil-rights groups argue that such legislation serves big business and the state, while providing little protection for workers. Indeed, in May 2015 the High Court ruled that workers who participated in strikes would be forced to take early retirement. However, this ruling would be difficult to implement in reality – according to the Egyptian Center for Economic and Social Rights, at least 1,655 labour protests and actions took place in 2014.

The labour sector continues to organise strikes. It demands the establishment of a freedom-of-association law (particularly for the establishment of trade unions), the improvement of living and employment standards, and the establishment of minimum and maximum wages.[23] One of the central demands of the uprising in 2011 was progress in social justice and economic development, but little has been made.[24]

Media

In the months after the uprising, there was a veritable explosion of media. New newspapers and media channels were established, and the media arena was the most open that Egyptians could remember. This atmosphere allowed far more discussion about major political and social issues than had previously been possible. A quintessential example is provided by political satirist Bassem Youssef, who became one of the most famous Arab media icons in modern times with his show *Al-Bernameg*, receiving an average of 40m viewers a week.

This opening also allowed for the promotion of more radical ideas from Islamist sources and the dissemination of more divisive commentary. Polarisation between Islamists and anti-Islamists affected the media. On both sides, news sources and media competed in progressively dehumanising the 'other', a trend that continued even after Morsi's removal from office.

Once the army had reasserted its authority in July 2013, one of its first steps was to take Islamist channels off the air. These channels undeniably incited violence, but such incitement against Islamists on rival channels continued unabated.

This was the first step towards a tightening of the public space that ensued. While the media generally support the new political dispensation in Cairo, dissent is barely tolerated or covered in the mainstream press. On the contrary, most media outlets show overwhelming bias, supporting the authorities and ensuring that a genuinely pluralistic public debate is absent.[25] The anti-government, pro-Islamist media – based outside Egypt – is incredibly problematic. Pro-Brotherhood stations, mostly based in Qatar or Turkey, often broadcast deeply sectarian diatribes, and provide platforms for inciting violence – examples have included Al-Jazeera Mubasher Misr (which the Qatari authorities eventually closed), Misr Alaan, Mukamaleen and others.

Under Sisi, the new constitution ostensibly ensures the media's freedom, but in practice legal restrictions continue to limit their activities, often in concert with constitutional limitations. The 2014 constitution provides for a new Supreme Council for the Regulation of Media, but it awaits legislation and the establishment of independent bodies that are meant to oversee state media.

In 2014 the cabinet drafted a new law that prohibited the publication of information related to the armed forces. This would affect print, radio and television outlets, as well as social media. The prohibition, in theory, would apply 'to analysis and investigative work, any statistics or data on military assets and strategy, and any other information that might harm the security of the members of the armed forces'.[26] As yet, there have been few reported cases that have come under this restriction. In August 2015, the cabinet introduced another counter-terrorism law that included articles allowing for the imposition of heavy financial penalties on journalists whose reports were deemed inaccurate by the government.

Opposition media were a target long before these laws were introduced, however. The most highly publicised case of government restrictions on press freedom has been the arrest of three Al-Jazeera English journalists in December 2013. The arrest was followed some time thereafter by a large international campaign calling for their release. On the one hand, this was a case about press freedoms; but on the other, analysts interpreted the case as a proxy war between Egypt's pro-military establishment and the Qatari state, which finances and runs the Al-Jazeera network. The three journalists were eventually released in 2015.[27] But the case serves as a reminder of the status of journalists in Egypt, with the number of journalists held in detention currently at an all-time high, and many of them reporting mistreatment in custody.

Examples include Mohamed Badr, an Al-Jazeera cameraman who was released after seven months of detention; Mahmoud Abu Zied, a freelance photojournalist who remains in detention; and Al-Jazeera's Abdullah al-Shami, who was freed after ten months, having carried out a partial hunger strike. Even Youssef was not spared, despite his international fame as the 'Arab Jon Stewart'. He cancelled his show in June 2014. This followed intense pressure and threats after he became increasingly critical of the new political order under Sisi. Facing a lawsuit, Youssef eventually left Egypt. Other television shows were cancelled after they made, or allowed guests to make, 'unpatriotic' comments.

None of this can be fully appreciated without understanding the broad layout of the Egyptian media, which is dominated by the state. There are more than 500 newspapers and print publications in Egypt, but the state owns several of the major titles.

The state controls all terrestrial broadcasting, which is the first source of information for Egyptian citizens, although there are a number of privately owned satellite channels with large audiences. While many point to the growth of social media as a source of information, internet penetration is still relatively low, and the use of Facebook and Twitter is still centred on a minority of the population.

Broadly speaking, many existing media outlets are particularly reluctant to criticise the government – sometimes out of fear and intimidation, but in other cases because they genuinely support the administration. Between 2011 and 2013, a large portion of the media, particularly those parts funded by the state, supported the military and its allies, or remained loyal to figures associated with the Mubarak regime. This is not entirely surprising because the media were a pillar of that system – a position they reclaimed with a great deal of enthusiasm in the post-Morsi era. Journalists who were supportive of the revolution that removed Mubarak came to view the Morsi government as an intrinsic threat, not only to dissent, but to their personal freedoms, and subsequently embraced Sisi.

Conclusion

Civil society expanded massively in the months following the 2011 revolution. Regrettably, the post-Morsi political order undid much of this progress as part of its 'war on terror'. That 'war' identifies not only radical-militant violence as a threat, but also any kind of dissent; civil-society groups, even though they are in no way violent, have suffered as a consequence.

Nevertheless, although the authorities may be popular and securely in power, they cannot always decisively constrain civil society. Youth groups are, by nature, difficult to control; civil-society organisations, especially human-rights groups, are experimenting with imaginative ways to manoeuvre around state control; and media outlets are becoming more critical.

The new government seems to believe it can control the growth of political consciousness; but in a country where the vast majority of people are under the age of 35, this may not be possible. Egypt's woes have grown. Whether this presages a new revolutionary quake is worth considering.

Notes

1 Sara Aggout, 'Unemployment Rates Reach 13.4% in 3Q in 2013', *Daily News Egypt*, 17 November 2013, http://www.dailynewsegypt.com/2013/11/17/unemployment-rates-reach-13-4-in-3q-2013/.

2 Holly Young, 'Egyptian Education System doesn't Prepare the Youth for Modern Jobs', *Guardian*, 20 August 2013, http://www.theguardian.com/global-development-professionals-network/2014/aug/20/youth-unemployment-interactive-salma-wahba.

3 As Gallup surveys indicated in the months after the uprising, only 8% of those who protested used Facebook or Twitter as a source of news. See H.A. Hellyer, 'Egyptians' Safety Fears Mount After Revolution', Gallup, 1 November 2011, http://www.gallup.com/poll/150467/egyptians-safety-fears-mount-revolution.aspx.

4 See 'Full English Translation of Egypt's New Protest Law', *Ahram Online*, 25 November 2013, http://english.ahram.org.eg/News/87375.aspx.

5 'Egypt: Generational Jail – Egypt's Youth Go from Protest to Prison', Amnesty International, 29 June 2015, available at https://www.amnesty.org/en/documents/mde12/1853/2015/en/.

6 Ahmed Fouad, 'Egypt's Youth "Have had Enough"', *Al Monitor*, 7 October 2014, translated by Pascale el-Khoury, http://www.al-monitor.com/pulse/originals/2014/10/youth-movements-egypt-crisis-state.html.

7 Mostafa Hashem, 'The Dangers of Alienating Egypt's Youth', Carnegie Endowment for International Peace, 6 March 2014, http://carnegieendowment.org/sada/?fa=54793.

8 *Ibid.*

9 The full text of the laws is available at http://www.icnl.org/research/library/files/Egypt/law84-2002-En.pdf.

10 *Ibid.*

11 The International Center for Not-for-Profit Law, 'NGO Law Monitor: Egypt', http://www.icnl.org/research/monitor/egypt.html.

12 H.A. Hellyer, 'The End of an Era for Egypt's NGOs', *Al Arabiya*, 10 November 2014, http://english.alarabiya.net/en/views/news/middle-east/2014/11/10/The-end-of-an-era-for-Egypt-s-NGOs.html.

13 Atlantic Council, 'Factbox: Everything You Needed to Know

about Egypt's UPR', 7 November 2014, http://www.atlanticcouncil.org/blogs/egyptsource/factbox-everything-you-need-to-know-about-egypt-s-upr.

14 FIDH, 'Egypt: Harassment and Restrictions to Freedom of Association against Several Human Rights Organisation', 11 June 2015, https://www.fidh.org/International-Federation-for-Human-Rights/north-africa-middle-east/egypt/egypt-harassment-and-restrictions-to-freedom-of-association-against.

15 According to Human Rights Watch, the law 'empowers the government to shut down any group virtually at will, freeze its assets, confiscate its property, reject nominees to its governing board, block its funding, or deny requests to affiliate with international organizations. The law does not indicate that nongovernmental organizations have the right to appeal the decision.' See Human Rights Watch, 'Egypt: Dissolution Ultimatum for Independent Groups', 30 August 2014, https://www.hrw.org/news/2014/07/14/egypt-draft-law-threatens-independent-organizations.

16 For a copy of the letter and a list of the signatories, see http://www.cihrs.org/wp-content/uploads/2014/09/Advocacy-letter-31-August-2014-FINAL.pdf.

17 For the official statement about the NGO law by the Ministry of Social Solidarity, see http://www.sis.gov.eg/En/Templates/Articles/tmpArticleNews.aspx?ArtID=79188#.VdTZR7KqpBd.

18 See 'NGO Law Monitor: Egypt', http://www.icnl.org/research/monitor/egypt.html.

19 Gary K. Busch, 'Challenges to Egyptian Labour', Ocnus.net, 18 January 2015, http://www.ocnus.net/artman2/publish/Editorial_10/Challenges%20To%20Egyptian%20Labour.shtml.

20 Joel Benin, 'The Rise of Egypt's Workers', Carnegie Endowment for International Peace, 28 June 2012, http://carnegieendowment.org/2012/06/28/rise-of-egypt-s-workers#.

21 Adham Youssef, 'Workers in Sisi's Egypt's: Muted by Promises of "Development"', *Daily News Egypt*, 11 June 2015, http://www.dailynewsegypt.com/2015/06/11/workers-in-al-sisis-egypts-muted-by-promises-of-development/.

22 *Ibid.*

23 El-Mahrousa Center for Socioeconomic Development, 'The Annual Report Brief on Labor Movement in Egypt', 2014, http://elmahrousacenter.org/english/wp-content/uploads/2015/01/The-Annual-Report-Brief-on-Labor-Movement-in-Egypt1.pdf.

24 Mai Shams El-Din, 'Human Rights in Focus: Nadim Mansour', Mada Masr, 26 April 2015, http://www.madamasr.com/sections/politics/human-rights-focus-nadeem-mansour.

25 Mohamed Elmeshad, 'We Completely Agree: Egyptian Media in the Era of President el-Sisi', Committee to Protect Journalists, available at https://cpj.org/2015/04/attacks-on-the-press-egyptian-media-in-the-era-of-president-el-sisi.php.

26 See Egypt's profile on Freedom House's website, available at https://freedomhouse.org/report/freedom-press/2015/egypt#.VdD5ZpOqqko.

27 'CPJ Welcomes Al-Jazeera Pardons, Calls for All Other Journalists in Egypt to be Freed', Committee to Protect Journalists, 23 September 2015, https://cpj.org/2015/09/cpj-welcomes-al-jazeera-pardons-calls-for-all-othe.php.

CHAPTER SEVEN

A revolution without a revolutionary foreign policy

Gamal Hassan

Egypt's foreign policy faced enormous challenges as a result of the Arab Spring and the toppling of President Hosni Mubarak, in February 2011. It had to adapt to an unprecedented domestic convulsion and a rapidly changing regional landscape. This chapter seeks to explain how Egypt responded to these challenges, arguing that elements of continuity were far more powerful than propensities for change. Post-revolutionary actors, namely the Supreme Council of the Armed Forces (SCAF), Muhammad Morsi and Abdel Fattah Al-Sisi, displayed foreign-policy preferences and behaviours that can be traced back to the paradigm established under Mubarak – particularly the final decade of his 30-year rule – and even his predecessors, Anwar Sadat and Gamal Abdel Nasser.

The chapter will first outline foreign policy under Nasser, Sadat and Mubarak. Although Egypt has parted with Nasser's ideological and strategic orientation, remnants of his doctrine have persisted, particularly the notion that the country should play a leading role in the region, which underlies the state's ethos and public discourse. It will then discuss Mubarak's doctrine, itself surprisingly influenced by Nasserist principles, with a focus on three key aspects: Egypt's relations with the Arab world, Israel–Palestine and the United States.

This analysis will demonstrate that, despite fluctuations, the principles of Mubarak's foreign policy remain intact four years after he was removed from power. During the 18-month SCAF-dominated transitional period, the fundamental orientations of Egypt's foreign policy did not change, despite pressure from revolutionary actors. The army's strict adherence to Mubarak's foreign policy highlighted its role as an architect of the policy and a stakeholder in the regional order. When Morsi came to power, in June 2012, he sought to use foreign policy as a means to consolidate his shaky and embattled regime, but he still resorted to Mubarak's playbook, discarding ideological considerations in favour of pragmatism. He exploited Egypt's role as a mediator between Israel and Hamas during the November 2012 conflict in Gaza the same way his predecessor had in the final six years of his tenure. Morsi's attempts to introduce changes to Egypt's regional posture were arguably limited to overtures to Tehran and closer relations with Turkey and Qatar. Finally, the overthrow of Morsi, in July 2013, and the ascendancy of Sisi set the stage for further consolidation of Mubarak's foreign-policy doctrine. The army now plays an increasingly central role in shaping foreign policy, and Egypt has become more dependent on an alliance with the Gulf countries, notably Saudi Arabia.

In response to new challenges, such as the menace Islamist militants pose throughout the Middle East, as well as threats to Egyptian water security arising from poor relations with the Nile Basin countries, Sisi has pursued a more active agenda than his predecessors. His outspokenness about the need to contain jihadist violence suggests that Egypt may take a leading role in protecting the regional order from the risk of collapse.

Egyptian foreign policy under Nasser, Sadat and Mubarak

Although subsequent leaders moved away from Nasser's foreign-policy doctrine, which was predicated on anti-colonialism, Arab nationalism and a leading role for Egypt in the Middle East, these ideas have remained relevant as ideals. The Nasserist outlook has not completely vanished from public opinion, state discourse or foreign-policy orientation, even if it no longer defines the official line. In particular, there is still a correlation between implementing an active and leading foreign policy in the region and maintaining the legitimacy of the regime. Even today, the sway and allure of a leadership role can easily be detected among Egypt's public and policy-makers.

This continues to be the case, despite the paradigm shift that followed Egypt's defeat in the 1967 war with Israel, which illustrated to the regime and the people the costliness of a leadership role in the region. Even Nasser's widely popular regime learnt that such a role could devastate its legitimacy rather than boost it. This simple, crucial fact would never escape his successors as they sought to articulate their own foreign policy. It played a significant role in Sadat's decision to engage in peace talks with Israel and establish a strategic, political and economic relationship with the US. Under Sadat, Egypt became a stakeholder in the global system of US alliances, rather than a challenger to the regional order, as it was under Nasser.

Mubarak worked within the parameters of Sadat's foreign policy, yet Nasserist ideals continued to influence his doctrine. This was evident in his insistence on maintaining a degree of independence vis-à-vis the US, ensuring that the relationship did not develop into a client–patron one. For example, Mubarak uncompromisingly refused to grant the US a permanent military base in Ras Banas, despite insistent requests from 1982 onwards, and despite the military receiving US$1.3 billion in annual aid from the US. Another example is Mubarak's refusal to visit Israel.[1]

Understanding Mubarak's doctrine is important to explaining the trends and dynamics in Egyptian foreign policy after the Arab Spring. Mubarak managed to set himself apart from his predecessors by adopting a consistent and largely predictable foreign policy that brought Egypt three decades of unprecedented stability and peace. It is best explained by looking at relations with the Arab world, Israel–Palestine and the US.

Mubarak had inherited an untenable legacy from Sadat. Cast aside by most Arab countries and suspended from the Arab League in 1979 as punishment for its separate peace with Israel, Egypt's regional standing hit an unprecedented low, which was bound to have dire consequences for the regime at home. The secular and Islamist opposition were likely to use the degradation of Egypt's status in the Arab world as ammunition against the regime. In response, Mubarak sought to mend fences in the region, focusing on the Gulf monarchies, which were home to millions of Egyptian expatriates who sent back remittances valuable to a cash-strapped economy. He successfully reintegrated Egypt into the Arab world in the late 1980s and restored severed diplomatic relations.

During the First Gulf War, Mubarak carved out a new role for Egypt as a stabilising force and keeper of the regional order. While alignment with the US-led international coalition was in drastic contrast to the Nasserist doctrine, it made Egypt indispensable to regional security arrangements. Mubarak harboured deep suspicions towards Iran's regional ambitions and tactics, consistently rebuffing its attempts to normalise relations with Egypt; for example, he rejected Iran's 2005 proposal to resume tourism to Egypt. Henceforth, the essence of Mubarak's foreign policy was an alliance with the Gulf monarchies, in particular Saudi Arabia, against Iran.

Yet Mubarak's openness to the Arab world drew a clear line between the peace treaty with Israel and other dynamics in the region. Deemed a vital strategic asset of unparalleled importance, the treaty weathered several wars in Lebanon and two Palestinian intifadas. It was vital for relations with the US, and with the inception of the peace process between Israel and the Palestinians in the 1990s, it gave Egypt regional leverage and international weight. The country's role as a mediator thus became a major theme in its diplomacy throughout the 1990s. Peace talks provided Mubarak with a chance to stress Egypt's importance to the regional order and US interests alike. While relations with Israel were a strategic liability in the 1980s, they became a valuable asset throughout the next two decades.

Gradually, relations between Egypt and Israel entered a new phase of strategic peace.[2] For example, during the war between Hizbullah and Israel in 2006, Mubarak, like Saudi Arabia, viewed the war as deliberately staged by the political party-cum-militia and Iranian proxy to boost its status. For the first time in the Arab–Israeli conflict, major Arab countries publicly denounced a resistance group that was facing fierce Israeli incursions. The fact that, significant opposition at home notwithstanding, Mubarak maintained his criticism of Hizbullah – in effect, siding with Israel – is a testament to the wide freedom of manoeuvre he enjoyed in formulating foreign policy, with a minimal price to pay domestically. Cementing the alliance with Saudi Arabia and preserving relations with Israel was apparently a policy worth pursuing, no matter how much criticism it drew at home.

Reactions to the December 2008–January 2009 war in Gaza between Israel and Hamas followed similar dynamics. However, as a result of its geographic proximity to the conflict and the controversial status of the Rafah border crossing, Egypt stood to lose more from siding with Israel against Hamas. In the midst of the war, Mubarak and his foreign minister Ahmad Abu el-Gheit made clear that Rafah would only be fully opened in accordance with the Rafah Agreement, a mechanism that Israel, the Palestinian Authority (PA) and the European Union established in November 2005. The agreement facilitated the movement of goods between Gaza and Egypt, under the auspices of the European Border Assistance Mission. The goal was to alleviate the humanitarian crisis in Gaza, which had become a source of embarrassment for both Egypt and Israel. This arrangement, however, was abolished after Hamas unilaterally seized Gaza in June 2007, and Israel imposed a blockade with support from Egypt and the PA.

Hamas built a network of tunnels running between Gaza and Sinai, which became central to Gaza's economy. Perversely, the tunnel economy created vested interests on both sides of the border. Although Egyptian authorities suspected that the tunnels were used to smuggle weapons into Sinai, they tolerated them to avoid a humanitarian catastrophe in Gaza, which could lead to a potential escalation. More importantly, this dangerous policy was designed to maintain leverage over Palestinian factions in Gaza. In a powerful expression of the government's determination, Gheit threatened in February 2008 to 'break the legs' of anyone who tried to use force to cross the border. Despite fierce domestic criticism of Egypt's role in the Israeli-imposed blockade against Gaza, Mubarak continued to cement ties with Israel, signing the Qualifying Industrial Zones agreement, as well as a controversial commercial gas deal.

Finally, Egypt's relationship with the US started to fracture in the aftermath of 9/11. The administration of George W. Bush started to make its annual economic aid to Egypt (US$200 million) conditional on human-rights and democratic reform. The US-led invasion of Iraq in 2003 complicated matters further, especially because Mubarak – backed by the military[3] – rebuffed numerous US requests to send Egyptian troops, even in symbolic numbers, to Iraq and Afghanistan. While the regional landscape was in flux, Mubarak kept to his old-style retroactive diplomacy. Unlike in his calculations during the First Gulf War, Mubarak gauged that Egypt stood nothing to gain from the 2003 war in Iraq. He preferred to drag his feet over reform, hoping that future US administrations would change course.

Towards the end of his rule, Mubarak's foreign policy largely centred on a conservative doctrine to maintain the status quo in the region. Even as he presided over Egypt's declining power, he manoeuvred to preserve a pivotal role for it in the region – one not at all commensurate with its relative decline. His exclusive fixation with regional policy, namely the strategic alliance with the Gulf states and the peace treaty with Israel, led to considerable retreat on other vital fronts, such as the African one, as discussed below. Yet Mubarak's foreign-policy doctrine would prove hard to reverse even after he was forced to step down and had exited the scene.

The challenges of the Arab Spring

Regional responses to the popular protests against Mubarak show how important his foreign-policy approach had become. Egypt's network of alliances feared a potential fragmentation of the regional order. Israel, for example, worried that Mubarak's departure would threaten the peace treaty and the stability that accompanied it. Both Prime Minister Benjamin Netanyahu and then-president Shimon Peres warned of a potential Islamist takeover, with Peres famously declaring, 'a fanatic religious oligarchy is not better than a lack of democracy'. Israeli officials and the Jewish lobby in the US thus campaigned persistently to dissuade President Barack Obama from abandoning Mubarak, arguing that it would send the wrong message to US allies in the region.[4]

Similarly, the Gulf states made no secret of their support for Mubarak. Secretary General of the Gulf Cooperation Council Abdullatif al-Zayani declared support for Egypt's stability against what the emir of Kuwait denounced as 'riots'. The foreign minister of the United Arab Emirates, Sheikh Abdullah bin Zayed al-Nahyan, visited Mubarak just two days before his ousting as a sign of unconditional support for the Egyptian regime.[5] But no country was more alarmed than Saudi Arabia, which following unprecedented collaboration with Egypt from 2006 onwards had come to view Mubarak as the bedrock of regional order. Mubarak's removal represented a setback for Saudi Arabia's regional posture in relation to Iran. A post-Mubarak era, whether Islamist or nationalist, did not bode well for the oil-rich kingdom. It inevitably conjured up memories of the role Egypt played under Nasser, who ended up in direct confrontation with Saudi Arabia in Yemen in the 1960s. Saudi Arabia was thus dismayed by the US calling on Mubarak to step down.

The combined pressures emanating from the region (Israel and the Gulf states) reportedly prompted the US administration to accept a transition that did not demand the immediate departure of Mubarak.[6] After all, they faced the possibility of Egypt revisiting its foreign-policy principles.

SCAF rule: forces of continuity vs inconsistent attempts at change

In one of its early statements upon assuming power, the SCAF vowed to respect all of Egypt's agreements and international treaties, alluding to the peace treaty with Israel. This statement diminished expectations of a fundamental change in foreign policy and reiterated the prominence of the army, particularly in relation to long-standing security arrangements with Israel. Regardless of events on the ground and emotions the peace treaty proved to be more deeply entrenched than many had expected. Both the SCAF and Netanyahu sought to keep the treaty and its security component intact.[7] They contained serious crises, such as the cross-border attacks on Eilat in southern Israel in August 2011, and the storming of the Israeli embassy in Cairo by an angry mob one month later. No viable alternative was offered to replace Mubarak's world view vis-à-vis Israel – after all, the head of the SCAF, Field Marshal Muhammad Tantawi, had been Mubarak's defence minister for 20 years.

Attempts to change the direction of Egyptian foreign policy under the SCAF were therefore limited and faced significant pushback. One week after Mubarak's fall, for example, Egypt allowed two Iranian ships to pass through the Suez Canal for the first time since 1979. A few months later, in an attempt to echo the revolutionary euphoria engulfing Egypt, newly appointed foreign minister Nabil el-Araby questioned the long diplomatic rupture between Egypt and Iran. He received an invitation to visit Tehran and declared that he intended to accept it, suggesting talks would take place to normalise relations between the two countries. The SCAF swiftly rebuffed the move, which had reportedly drawn the ire of Tantawi personally.[8] Changing the direction of foreign policy at such a delicate transitional moment was perceived as reckless. Araby instead visited Saudi Arabia, as did Prime Minister Essam Sharaf, in an attempt to assuage Saudi concerns about cordial signals to Tehran. Forces of continuity were apparently deeply entrenched, and capable of withstanding light winds of change. The episode revealed that the SCAF had the final say on fundamental foreign-policy issues, as it had assumed the prerogatives of the top position after replacing Mubarak. The foreign ministry's role was largely confined to carrying out policy, particularly when it came to major decisions.

Although revolutionary actors were resentful of certain foreign-policy decisions, the SCAF still managed to weather public opinion during this delicate time. Relations with Saudi Arabia were one source of contention. The poor conditions in which 1.2m Egyptians worked in Saudi Arabia were seen as an illustration and indictment of the Mubarak government's subservient attitude towards the Gulf monarchy. The case of an Egyptian lawyer jailed in Saudi Arabia triggered protests in front of the Saudi embassy in Cairo in April 2012, after which the Saudi ambassador was recalled to Riyadh for consultations. The prime minister and the SCAF issued apologies and called for his return, and a high-level delegation of public figures from across the spectrum visited Saudi Arabia for the same purpose. By May, the ambassador was back in Cairo.[9] The episode showed that many players in Cairo had a stake in the powerful alliance forged with the Gulf states.

In contrast to its robust and largely consistent policy towards the Gulf countries and Israel, Egypt was about to reap the dire harvest of years of neglect of Africa, and in particular the Nile Basin countries, which occupy a region similarly vital to Egypt's national security. In April 2011, amid much fanfare, the Ethiopian government began construction on the Grand Ethiopian Renaissance Dam (GERD) on the Blue Nile, which was meant to hold 74bn cubic metres of water. The Ethiopian declaration followed intractable negotiations between Egypt and the ten riparian countries of the Nile Basin. The talks, which had dragged on since 2005, came to a dead end when five Nile Basin countries signed in May 2010 a framework agreement despite vociferous objections from Egypt and Sudan.[10] Egypt insisted on the sanctity of previous agreements[11] and on 'historical rights', but its stance had proved untenable in the face of the increasingly fierce opposition of upstream countries, led by Ethiopia. As a result, Egypt suspended its membership in the Nile Basin Initiative.[12]

Ethiopia has long challenged what it considers Egyptian control of the Nile Basin water resources. The GERD, therefore, was not only a massive hydropower project (expected to generate 6,000 megawatts annually), but also a tool of domestic legitimacy and regional clout. Ethiopia maintained that it was exercising its right to use its water resources, and criticised Egypt's extravagant consumption of Nile water.[13] Egypt, however, stressed that it was already in an era of water poverty. It has persistently argued that the Nile is its only source of water, whereas Ethiopia gets 122bn cubic metres of surface water annually from 12 water basins. Furthermore, out of the 1,600bn cubic metres that flow into the Basin every year, only 84bn cubic metres becomes river flow in Aswan, of which only two-thirds is allocated to Egypt.[14]

The GERD project marked a turning point in Nile Basin politics. Egypt found itself increasingly isolated, facing a new reality on the ground. The diplomatic impasse with the Nile Basin countries, compounded by the GERD, illustrates the nature of diplomatic challenges facing Egypt in the post-Mubarak era. Such challenges were essentially a direct result of Mubarak's fixation on regional politics and relations with the US at the expense of other significant issues.

Foreign policy under Morsi

When Morsi, the Muslim Brotherhood's candidate, was elected president in June 2012, some anticipated a dramatic shift in foreign policy. The challenge the Brotherhood had to meet was how to balance its ideological platform with the obligations of governance. Although its short-lived rule makes it difficult to discern a clear pattern in the Brotherhood's foreign-policy approach, Morsi's year in power indicated strong elements of continuity.

While in opposition, the Brotherhood had relentlessly attacked Mubarak's foreign policy and his alliances, focusing in particular on the peace treaty with Israel and the client-like relationship with the US. Brotherhood-affiliated figures had referred to Mubarak as a 'Zionist agent' for his role in the controversial Gaza blockade. Morsi's rise to power was accordingly expected to affect the relationship between Egypt and Israel. Instead, Morsi publicly stressed his government's commitment to the peace treaty – indeed, even before he was elected – stating that 'Egypt has institutions that respect the treaties signed in the past, as long as the parties are committed to them as part of honouring sovereignty and independence'. He reiterated this position in subsequent months.[15] Other Brotherhood leaders maintained their anti-Israel rhetoric, but left the actual conduct of foreign policy unchallenged. For example, the head of the Brotherhood's political wing, Saad al-Katatny, praised a demonstrator who removed Israel's flag from the embassy in Cairo during the September 2011 crisis, but was conspicuously silent on Morsi's 'business as usual' approach.

Challenging the regional order turned out to be more difficult than expected. The security triangle of Egypt, Israel and the US proved to be a powerful strategic reality that was difficult to overlook and almost impossible to overturn. Morsi's calculations were influenced by dependence on annual US military aid (around US$2bn), coupled with the Brotherhood's need for US political support. More importantly, he came to realise that relations between Egypt and Israel operate through security channels that bypass even the president.

This reality became particularly evident during the brief round of clashes between Israel and Hamas in November 2012, which was Morsi's first foreign-policy test. Conscious of the limitations and aware of the risks, he sought to score political points by mediating a ceasefire, just as Mubarak-era officials had. Morsi thus came to realise that the 'Israeli connection' might be a political asset. Yearning for international approval, he used his role as mediator to present himself to the West as a moderate and trustworthy player.

While in public Morsi could capitalise on the Brotherhood's historic relations with Hamas, appearing to be on the Palestinian group's side, he had to depend on the same team that had served under Mubarak in the Egyptian intelligence service, which had long-standing relations with its Israeli counterpart. In doing so, he gave the intelligence service his stamp of approval in managing complex relations with Israel.[16] Morsi's relations with the Palestinian group were similarly convoluted: for example, like Mubarak, he cracked down on Hamas's smuggling activities in Rafah, and flooded the tunnels with sewage in early 2013 to restrict the flow of weapons between Gaza and Sinai.[17]

Relations with the Gulf countries also posed challenges. The Brotherhood had forged close financial and political ties with Qatar, a major patron of Islamists in the region. This adversely affected relations with Saudi Arabia and the UAE, both increasingly alarmed by the ascendancy of the populist Islamist party. Historical rivalry between Saudi Arabia and Qatar added to the complexity.

Morsi's expressed willingness to reach out to Tehran further complicated matters with the Gulf states. In September 2012, one month after attending a summit of the Non-Aligned Movement in Tehran, Morsi stressed the need to engage with Iran to resolve the Syrian crisis. It was the first visit to Iran by an Egyptian president since the Islamic Revolution, in 1979, and was followed by a trip by then Iranian president Mahmoud Ahmadinejad to Cairo in February 2013, during which he called for a strategic alliance with Egypt. However limited, Morsi's opening toward Tehran exacerbated Saudi and Emirati anxiety about a regional realignment.

While Morsi may have assumed that modest overtures to Tehran could balance Egypt's relations with the Gulf countries

and give Cairo more room for manoeuvre, it merely alienated historical allies. For the Gulf countries, the Iranian threat
loomed large, and warding off Iranian expansionism – through
Shia proxies in Syria, Iraq and Lebanon – was a major concern.
In this tense regional environment, the Gulf monarchies saw
regional dynamics in terms of rigid sectarian-based alignments, and accordingly viewed Egypt's natural place as being
in the Sunni camp. Morsi's overtures to Tehran and policy of
neutrality were therefore a source of deep frustration, and even
trepidation, for Saudi Arabia and the UAE.[18]

Morsi also fostered closer relations with Turkey, which
invested heavily in his government and became another
significant regional patron.[19] The Brotherhood viewed Recep
Tayyip Erdogan's Justice and Development Party (AKP) as
a role model and source of inspiration, particularly regarding its experience with democracy and governance. A speech
by Erdogan at Cairo University in November 2012, pledging
support for the new Egyptian democracy and solidarity with
the Palestinians in Gaza, outlined a regional vision that emphasised strong cooperation with Egypt.

This was in contrast to relations with the Mubarak government, which had been marked by a sense of rivalry since the
meteoric rise of the AKP and Erdogan in 2002. The implications of this new experiment in cohabitation between Islamism
and democracy were not lost on the Mubarak regime. In fact,
Erdogan's regional ambitions and active foreign policy, particularly with regard to Gaza and the Palestinian cause, were
infringing on what Cairo has long considered its domain.

Nevertheless, Morsi failed to steer Egyptian foreign policy
in a new direction. This chapter has demonstrated that, despite
small-scale attempts to recalibrate foreign policy, Morsi's
policies were by no means a clean break with the fundamental principles laid out by Mubarak. Morsi acted within the

contours of Egypt's major alliances, particularly regarding the US and Israel – the area that had been the subject of decades of strident criticism from the Brotherhood. Moreover, throughout his presidency, Morsi did not alter the army's significant role in defining and pursuing the Egyptian national interest.

30 June and beyond: business as usual?

While the replacement of Morsi with a military-backed regime in July 2013 was essentially a product of intense domestic polarisation, it was also influenced by regional dynamics. Regional actors, notably Saudi Arabia and the UAE, buttressed this political transformation, supporting the rise of Sisi. The regional order, in which Cairo, Riyadh and Abu Dhabi were deeply invested, became the fundamental guarantor of the new regime's legitimacy in Cairo. Four years after the Arab Spring, Mubarak's doctrine and the alliances he managed to forge throughout his rule stand out as the major pillars of Egyptian foreign policy.[20]

Having perceived the Brotherhood's rule as a threat, the Gulf countries rushed to embrace the new regime and became its main patrons, providing economic assistance and political support. The day after Morsi had been removed from power, Saudi King Abdullah bin Abdul Aziz Al Saud congratulated the new interim president, Adly Mansour, adding that the armed forces had 'led Egypt out of a dark tunnel only God knows how dangerous its implications would have been'. A few days later, Saudi Arabia, Kuwait and the UAE pledged US$12bn in 'urgent' economic aid to Egypt.

The Gulf monarchies unequivocally sided with the new regime. Their support was essential to shield it from Western (and other) criticism and, at times, rehabilitate it. Its legitimacy was at stake, especially after the violent dispersal of two sit-ins in Cairo in August 2013 resulted in widespread international condemnation. Saudi Arabia's decisive diplomatic counter-offensive arguably rescued the new regime from international isolation. King Abdullah made a rare public statement in August 2013 stressing support for Egypt against 'those who try to interfere with its domestic affairs', while foreign minister Prince Saud al-Faisal argued vehemently against punishing Egypt. Egypt also grew closer to the UAE, which quickly became a crucial ally of the new regime. Sisi later vowed that the security of the Gulf would be a chief priority for his government, going as far as to publicly state that the army would be ready to intervene to fend off any security threats facing the Gulf states.[21]

The Obama administration's response to the new regime in Cairo was ambivalent, and it was unable to decide whether to view Egypt as a strategic ally or an untrustworthy dictatorship.[22] The US criticised the deadly crackdowns in August 2013 and cancelled *Operation Bright Star*, a joint biannual military exercise. In October 2013, the US recalibrated its aid package to Egypt, announcing a temporary freeze on military assistance that included *Apache* attack helicopters, *Harpoon* missiles, M1-A1 tank parts and F-16 warplanes, as well as US$260m.[23]

The move suggested that relations between the two countries now hinged on the Egyptian regime's record on democratisation and human rights. This suggested a clean break with the strategic interests on which their partnership had rested since the mid-1970s: access to the Suez Canal, military overflights and, most importantly, strict observance of the Camp David Accords with Israel. All other issues, including human rights and democratic reform, had been of secondary significance. A shift in the foundations of such a partnership was bound to unsettle the regional order and upset its principal stakeholders.[24]

But the break did not come to pass. After a prolonged congressional debate, the US sent the *Apache* helicopters to assist Egypt's war against jihadist groups in Sinai. In April 2015, it released the other previously withheld weapons systems: 12 F-16 jets, 12 *Harpoon* missiles and as many as 125 *Abrams* tank kits. Obama decided, however, to end the policy of cash-flow financing, which was essential for the army to buy weapons on credit using future aid. In August, Cairo and Washington resumed the 'Strategic Dialogue' after a nine-year hiatus. Such developments point to a realisation that alienating Egypt does not serve US interests, particularly in light of regional upheavals, such as the ascendancy of the Islamic State of Iraq and al-Sham (ISIS) and the fragmentation of Libya.

Besides an escalating Islamist insurgency in Sinai, pressure from regional allies also contributed to the reversal of the US position. Allies expressed deep concerns over the decision to curtail aid to Cairo. Faisal, for example, pledged to support the Egyptian military in the place of the US. Meanwhile, an Israeli minister said he was 'troubled by how decisions of this kind were liable to be interpreted in Egypt', arguing that they carried a 'risk of consequences for relations with Israel'.[25] Just as in February 2011, such vocal support for Egypt's new regime illustrated the deep entrenchment of Mubarak's regional doctrine and its importance to strategic realities. Strategic peace with Israel over time became a robust element of Egypt's network of alliances, and was even more critical than the country's relationship with the US guarantor, which had enabled the strategic peace in the first place.

In addition, Sisi appeared intent on sending signals to the US and other Western powers that Egypt was not lacking in strategic options, notably by developing military relations with Russia. In November 2013, Russia's defence and foreign ministers visited Egypt, the first time a joint visit at this level had taken place since the early 1970s. In February 2014, while still minister of defence, but widely regarded as Egypt's most powerful leader, Sisi visited Moscow with then-foreign minister Nabil Fahmy and a high-level military delegation. He made another visit as president in August. Such encounters were meant to facilitate arms deals with Russia, with reports of negotiations for a preliminary deal worth US$3.5bn.[26] Sisi also upgraded defence relations with France, acquiring *Rafale* fighter aircraft in February 2015. He has since explored other potential arms deals with Paris.

It is still premature to gauge the implications of this new orientation.[27] But this new approach is nevertheless reminiscent of a yearning for the more autonomous foreign policy of the Nasser era. Admittedly, circumstances have changed greatly since the 1960s, but Egypt's preference for maintaining balanced relations with the US remains strong.

New challenges

Regional instability, such as that caused by the emergence and expansion of militant groups, has created fresh challenges. In his speech before the United Nations General Assembly in September 2014, Sisi defined Islamist extremism as the main threat to the region's security, adding that 'Egypt will never walk away from its responsibility toward the region, and will work to restore the cohesiveness of the regional system'. Clearly, Egypt under Sisi continues to view its role as the ultimate guarantor of the status quo in the region, and is likely to remain part of the robust, albeit informal, alliance with Saudi Arabia, the UAE, Jordan and, tacitly, Israel. In the manner of Mubarak, Sisi is expected to view this alliance as a cornerstone of his foreign policy.

At the same time, the struggle with the Brotherhood and other jihadist movements is the government's primary concern. Egypt perceives the region in terms of a struggle between two rival camps: Islamists and anti-Islamists. The Islamists are considered to be one bloc, which may contain different colours but ultimately shares the same virulent ideology and goals. According to this world view, governments that support the Brotherhood, such as Turkey and Qatar, are dangerous adversaries. The tendency to lump different strains of political Islam into one group is a direct consequence of the life-and-death domestic struggles with the Brotherhood and Sinai-based group Ansar Bayt al-Maqdis. This rigid approach (which is understandable in current circumstances) will probably limit Egypt's room for manoeuvre in regional politics.

It has, for example, affected the alliance with Saudi Arabia. Although the Saudi government helped neutralise the Brotherhood in Egypt, it later started to show flexibility in its position towards the group, particularly after King Salman's ascension to the throne in January 2015. Saudi Arabia has prioritised cementing a Sunni camp to fend off Iran's Shia proxies, and has completely focused on the civil wars in Yemen, Syria and Iraq. To that end, the intervention against the Houthis in Yemen that began in March demonstrated Saudi Arabia's willingness to employ military tools to deter Iran and its proxies. This is a policy line that Egypt may not be willing or able to follow, beyond lending its rhetorical support. Egypt does not see itself as party to the sectarian conflicts ravaging the Levant, and does not view the Iranian threat in sectarian terms – Shias are a negligible minority in Egypt – but from the perspective of the balance of power.

Egypt's war of words with Turkey is another obstacle to an expanded Sunni alliance. Turkey – and Erdogan in particular – has insisted on refusing to acknowledge the Sisi government's legitimacy, describing the events of July 2013 as an illegitimate military coup. This is most probably a result of Erdogan's own struggle with the Turkish military: the ousting of Morsi mirrors the coup against the Islamist government in Turkey in 1997. Turkey therefore hosts Brotherhood-affiliated television channels that broadcast virulent criticism of Sisi and incite violence against his government.

On the Israeli–Palestinian front, Sisi faces greater complexity. After the renewal of hostilities between Hamas and Israel in July 2014, Egypt played its traditional role of mediator, with Sisi deriving political benefits as his predecessors had. However, he only did so after watching Hamas receive powerful blows from Israel. Indeed, the Palestinian faction's alignment with the Brotherhood, Sisi's sworn enemy, has brought Egypt's threat assessments even closer to those of Israel. The decision by an Egyptian court to declare Hamas a terrorist organisation in February 2015 marked Cairo's determination to further isolate the group and deal with it as an imminent threat; the decision was later reversed, though the warning was unmistakable. In contrast with Mubarak, who was strongly criticised for his ties with Israel and antagonism toward Hamas, Sisi benefited from a hardening of Egyptian public opinion against the Brotherhood and, by extension, Hamas. The shift may be linked to countless Egyptian media reports suggesting that there is a direct link between Hamas and the jihadist insurgency in Sinai, which has escalated since 2014.

The fragmentation of Libya also poses serious challenges, especially because of the porous 1,000-kilometre border the country shares with Egypt. Since it held elections in June 2014, Libya has witnessed rising conflict between Islamist and nationalist militias. With two governments claiming legitimacy, one in Tripoli and the other in Tobruk, Libya is rapidly approaching state failure. Egypt and the UAE have actively supported Tobruk, and the forces of General Khalifa Haftar, who in May 2014 launched a military operation aimed at ridding eastern Libya of jihadists. After Haftar called on Sisi to use 'all necessary military actions inside Libya' to secure its borders, Egypt and the UAE conducted covert military operations in August inside Libya. In February 2015, Egypt bombed ISIS affiliates in the coastal cities of Derna and Sirte, following the beheading of 21 Coptic Christians. These incidents indicate Sisi's assertiveness in responding to regional threats.

Water security and relations with Ethiopia will probably also occupy policymakers in coming years. In 2013 and 2014, Ethiopia seemed to drag its feet on lengthy technical negotiations over the operation of the GERD. An international panel of experts published in May 2013 a report that recommended further studies to assess the impact of the project on downstream countries,[28] but Ethiopia refused to suspend construction until negotiations had concluded. It has stressed that, as a matter of sovereignty, the operation of the GERD is non-negotiable. Egypt responded by withdrawing from the negotiations in January 2014. However, its position grew weaker as Ethiopia managed to win the support of Sudan, which probably has much to gain from the GERD, thus undermining the unity of the downstream countries.

Sisi's government seems inclined to reach a diplomatic solution to the dispute with Ethiopia. A joint declaration issued by Sisi and Ethiopian Prime Minister Hailemariam Desalegn in June 2014 stressed cooperation and dialogue to reach a settlement, though it failed to produce real changes. A new political intervention in March 2015 sought to break the stalemate. Egypt, Ethiopia and Sudan met in Khartoum and announced a joint declaration that addressed some of Egypt's concerns about the GERD's operation, suggesting a new cooperative environment. However, the statement did not deal with the GERD's storage capacity – which Ethiopia says is not open to discussion – and made no mention of Egypt's historical rights, thereby leaving many issues unresolved.

Experts are divided over the degree of harm the dam will inflict on Egypt in terms of its water share,[29] but there is a consensus that changes to the specifications of the project are necessary to the country's vital interests. A lot will depend on the operation of the GERD and its filling strategy for the first time. In any event, Egypt will need to comprehensively restructure its relations with not only Ethiopia but also Sudan and the upstream countries, to create a more favourable and cooperative strategic framework.

Conclusion

Nasser embraced Arab nationalism to carve out a leading role for his country in the Middle East. But defeat in 1967 and the subsequent peace treaty with Israel left an indelible mark on Egypt's foreign-policy orientation. Ambitions for regional leadership have not entirely subsided but rather have taken on different forms, in line with Egypt's transformation into a status quo power bent on preserving the regional order.

Throughout his 30-year rule, Mubarak sought to bolster Egypt's informal alliance with the Gulf countries and the strategic peace with Israel as a basis for an enhanced role for Egypt in the region, and also as a bridge to the US-led international system. Under Mubarak, Cairo was no longer a trendsetter in the Middle East, but a bedrock of regional stability. Near the end of his rule, Mubarak tilted more towards his regional partners and away from the US. This ultimately provided the basis for Egypt's network of alliances and established its position in the regional realignment that is currently unfolding. Counter-intuitively, the trends that prevailed in Egypt's foreign policy under Mubarak continued even after his removal from power. The revolutionary wave that swept the country did not result in a revolutionary foreign policy.

This is partly because the army has retained an unparalleled role in articulating and pursuing national interests. That role was challenged in the aftermath of the January 2011 uprising, particularly with the subsequent rise of the Brotherhood. Nevertheless, the army ensured that, even under Morsi's presidency, Egypt's alliances and orientation were kept intact. No political force in Egypt was capable of offering an alternative outline for a foreign policy that would constitute a clean break with the past, let alone of putting it into action.

With the overthrow of Morsi in 2013, the army's status was enhanced domestically and regionally. The alliance Mubarak had forged with the Gulf states and the strategic peace he kept with Israel stood out as the main sources of political and economic support for the military-backed regime that emerged in the aftermath of Morsi's ousting. Egypt under Sisi is likely to follow the path it did under Mubarak. But the challenges of containing jihadist violence across the region, coupled with a deepening of the Iranian threat to the Gulf states, might lead to a more proactive Egyptian policy primarily geared towards preserving the regional order.

Notes

1 Mubarak visited Israel once to offer his condolences for Rabin's assassination in 1995. His participation in the funeral came after heavy diplomatic pressure from the US.

2 Amnon Aran and Rami Ginat, 'Revisiting Egyptian Foreign Policy towards Israel under Mubarak: From Cold Peace to Strategic Peace', *Journal of Strategic Studies*, vol. 37, no. 4, August 2014, pp. 553–83.

3 US Embassy in Cairo, 'Defense Minister Tantawi on Iran, Iraq, Hamas, Sudan and FMF', 11 April 2006, WikiLeaks, https://wikileaks.org/plusd/cables/06CAIRO2183_a.html.

4 Amr Yossef, 'Israel and the Tahrir Revolution', in Dan Tschirgi, Walid Kazziha and Sean F. McMahon (eds), *Egypt's Tahrir Revolution* (Boulder, CO: Lynne Rienner, 2013), p. 212.

5 Yasmine Farouk, 'More than Money: Post-Mubarak Egypt, Saudi Arabia, and the Gulf', Gulf Research Center, April 2014, http://www.grc.net/download_generic.php?file_name=ODQwNjM%3D.

6 Mark Landler and Helene Cooper, 'Allies Press U.S. to Go Slow on Egypt', *New York Times*, 8 February 2011, http://www.nytimes.com/2011/02/09/world/middleeast/09diplomacy.html?_r=0.

[7] Gamal Abuel Hassan, 'Morsi and Netanyahu: Business as Usual', *Al-Monitor*, 4 April 2013, http://www.al-monitor.com/pulse/originals/2013/04/morsi-netanyahu-security-relationship.html#.

[8] Ahmed Aboul Gheit, *Shahadti: al-Siyasa al-Kharijia al-Misryya 2004–2011* (Cairo: Nahdat Misr, 2013), p. 402.

[9] Farouk, 'More than Money', p. 8.

[10] Only three countries (Ethiopia, Rwanda and Tanzania) had ratified the treaty as of May 2015.

[11] Egypt's historical rights to Nile water, including its annual share (55.5 bn cubic metres), are safeguarded by two treaties signed with Britain and Sudan, in 1929 and 1959. The upstream countries have long rejected the treaties as non-binding, claiming they unjustly and exclusively serve Egypt's interests, and that they are essentially colonial agreements because many countries were not yet independent when they were made. The validity of these treaties is controversial because international law upholds the principle of the succession of states.

[12] A regional framework established in 1999 aimed to encourage cooperation between upstream and downstream countries in the Nile Basin.

[13] To cope with its water-scarcity problem, some experts argue that Egypt has to change its water-use policies and transform its crop structure to reduce the area allocated to water-intensive crops such as rice. Agriculture accounts for only 14% of Egypt's GDP, but consumes 85% of its water resources. Almost one-third of the population works in agriculture.

[14] Rawia Tawfik, 'Revisiting Hydro-hegemony from a Benefit-Sharing Perspective: The Case of the Grand Ethiopian Renaissance Dam', German Development Institute, May 2015, https://www.die-gdi.de/uploads/media/DP_5.2015.pdf.

[15] Liad Porat, 'The Muslim Brotherhood and Egypt–Israel Peace', *Mideast Security and Policy Studies*, no. 102, 1 August 2013, http://besacenter.org/mideast-security-and-policy-studies/the-muslim-brotherhood-and-egypt-israel-peace/.

[16] Hassan, 'Morsi and Netanyahu'.

[17] Paul Taylor and Yasmine Saleh, 'Egypt Flooded Tunnels to Cut Gaza Arms Flow: Aide', Reuters, 18 February 2013, http://www.reuters.com/article/2013/02/18/us-palestinians-tunnels-egypt-idUSBRE91H0JA20130218.

[18] In June 2013, only a few days before his ousting, Morsi tried to reverse this policy by calling for a jihad in Syria against Assad, but it was already too late.

[19] By the end of 2012, trade between Egypt and Turkey was worth US$5.2bn. Turkish investments in Egypt amounted to US$1.9bn, with a target of $5bn. Moreover, Turkey provided Egypt with an assistance package worth US$2bn. See Azzurra Meringolo, 'From Morsi to Al-Sisi: Foreign Policy in the Service of Domestic Policy', *Insight Egypt*, no. 8, March 2015, available at http://www.iai.it/sites/default/files/inegypt_08.pdf.

[20] Gamal Abuel Hassan, 'Egypt's Foreign Policy Summed up

21 in One Sentence!', Dotmsr, 28 October 2014, http://dotmsr.com/ar/201/1/111889/#.VGjYVfldVFM.

21 'Sisi Praises Saudi Arabia, Vows Strong Gulf Ties', Al Arabiya, 24 May 2014, http://english.alarabiya.net/en/News/middle-east/2014/05/24/Sisi-praises-Saudi-Arabia-vows-strong-Gulf-ties.html.

22 Eric Trager, 'Obama Wrecked U.S.–Egypt Ties', Washington Institute for Near East Policy, 7 April 2015, http://www.washingtoninstitute.org/policy-analysis/view/obama-wrecked-u.s.-egypt-ties.

23 Michael R. Gordon and Mark Landler, 'In Crackdown Response, U.S. Temporarily Freezes Some Military Aid to Egypt', New York Times, 9 October 2013, http://www.nytimes.com/2013/10/10/world/middleeast/obama-military-aid-to-egypt.html?pagewanted=all&_r=0.

24 Tally Helfont, 'Slashed US Aid to Egypt and the Future of the Bilateral Relations', Institute for National Security Studies, 13 October 2013, http://www.inss.org.il/index.aspx?id=4538&articleid=5781.

25 Herb Keinon, Michael Wilner and Ariel Ben Solomon, 'Israeli Officials Say Egypt Peace Treaty is Paramount amid US Decision to Cut Cairo Aid', Jerusalem Post, 11 November, 2013, http://www.jpost.com/Middle-East/Israeli-officials-say-Egypt-peace-treaty-is-paramount-amid-US-decision-to-cut-Cairo-aid-328501.

26 David Schenker and Eric Trager, 'Egypt's Arms Deal with Russia: Potential Strategic Costs', Washington Institute for Near East Policy, 4 March 2014, http://www.washingtoninstitute.org/policy-analysis/view/egypts-arms-deal-with-russia-potential-strategic-costs.

27 Ephraim Kam and Zvi Magen, 'The New Contacts between Egypt and Russia: How Far Will They Go?', Institute for National Security Studies, 27 February 2014, http://www.inss.org.il/index.aspx?id=4538&articleid=6685.

28 The panel comprises experts from the three eastern Nile Basin countries (Egypt, Ethiopia and Sudan), in addition to four international experts.

29 Muhammed Nasr el-Din Allam, The Ethiopian Renaissance Dam Crisis: A Political Question or a Technical Problem? (Cairo: Al-Mahrousa Center for Publication and Information, 2014).

CHAPTER EIGHT

Militarisation and security challenges in Egypt

Hebatalla Taha

Egypt faces intensifying security challenges on three different 'fronts': a full-blown war between the army and insurgent *takfiri*[1] groups in North Sinai; an escalating Islamist insurgency across the rest of the country that has increasingly affected urban areas; and the threat of spillover from the civil war in Libya, where Egyptian forces have undertaken unilateral military action. While these challenges have affected stability and the standing of the government, and contributed to a nationwide sense of insecurity, they fundamentally differ in terms of their roots, nature and potency.

Since the rise to power of General Abdel Fattah Al-Sisi in July 2013, and the declaration of a 'war on terror', these challenges have been presented as interlinked and to be addressed simultaneously. The state has relied primarily on a military response, which has been depicted as the only solution to these existential crises and used to mobilise support and marginalise dissent. Such militarisation reflects not only the military's disproportionate dominance of the political space and state resources (as has been the case since 1952), but also a systemic preference for the use of force over other tools of governance

– whether at home or abroad – to achieve political objectives; and the elevation of the military as the unchallenged guardian of the nation.

This security-first approach, devoid of genuine outreach towards key dissenting or discontented groups in Egyptian society, has inadvertently engendered a predictable rise in violence, both individual and organised, and has led to the neglect of socio-economic and political issues. The approach has sent a message of exclusion, resulting in a dehumanising discourse on armed groups, civilians caught in the crossfire and all political opponents linked to a loosely defined 'Islamism'. The government's heavy-handedness is likely to cause a further backlash because it undermines Sisi's ability to deliver on the basic promises of his mandate to re-establish political and economic stability. This chapter argues that, although Egypt currently faces unprecedented security challenges, which regional instability has exacerbated, the upsurge in violence since 2013 is also linked to the militarisation of the state.

This chapter will outline each of the three security challenges, the factors underlying the expansion of violence, and the ways in which the state has assessed and responded to this violence. The project of militarisation is evident in each case. The chapter will subsequently discuss the configuration of the militarised state, the ways in which it places different threats under the all-encompassing umbrella of 'Islamism', and its use of regional dynamics, particularly the emergence of the Islamic State of Iraq and al-Sham (ISIS), in the service of its security posture.

North Sinai: between militant and military violence

The largest militant group operating in North Sinai, Ansar Bayt al-Maqdis (ABM), emerged following the 2011 uprising and has thrived on pervasive insecurity. One of its first attacks after

President Hosni Mubarak's resignation was on a controversial pipeline in North Sinai, which supplied natural gas to Israel at a cost below the market price. ABM subsequently widened its range of targets to include state infrastructure in the region, Israel, international peacekeepers, tourists in South Sinai and those it accused of 'collaborating' with the Egyptian government and Israeli intelligence service Mossad. This provoked military responses from each of the post-revolutionary governments: *Operation Eagle* under the Supreme Council of the Armed Forces (SCAF) in August 2011, *Operation Sinai* under president Muhammad Morsi one year later and a reboot of *Operation Sinai* under Sisi from mid-2013 onwards.

The deteriorating security situation in Sinai was a major factor behind Sisi's appointment as defence minister in August 2012. A group of *takfiris* stormed a military base and killed 16 soldiers, who had just sat down for their iftar meal. The incident elicited a public outcry, and Morsi took the opportunity to dismiss the unpopular Field Marshall Muhammad Tantawi and replace him with Sisi, whom many regarded as more sympathetic to the Brotherhood. When Sisi overthrew Morsi less than a year later, insecurity in Sinai galvanised public support in his favour. The military strongman was viewed as the only figure with the capacity to stamp out the threat from armed groups. However, armed activity in North Sinai escalated into a full-blown insurgency against the state, and *takfiris* have attacked state infrastructure and the armed forces with increasing vigour. Hundreds of soldiers and around 1,500 'militants' have died in successive military operations.[2]

The sense of lawlessness that prevails in Sinai dates back to the 1980s and 1990s, following the Camp David Peace Accords with Israel, which stipulated a reduced military presence in the peninsula. Because of this demilitarisation clause, the army was never fully in control of Sinai. Increased deployment of troops from 2012 onwards was designed to tackle the security vacuum. This was predicated on coordinating with Israel, which has accepted a larger military presence in Sinai to combat militant activity.

On Israel's periphery, the peninsula has suffered from economic and political neglect, resulting in a thriving smuggling business and other illicit activities. The Bedouin population has complained of inadequate basic services, such as water infrastructure and schools, evidence in their eyes of systematic political exclusion. Many say they are treated as second-class citizens: they are unable to register their property, while the majority are denied employment in the police, the army, the judiciary and the diplomatic service. These adversarial relations have historically facilitated the emergence of armed groups, and Sinai has undergone various waves of *takfiri* violence since the 1990s. ABM is thought to have subsumed the smaller *takfiri* groups into a coherent structure.

ABM is most active in an area that encompasses the cities of Rafah, Sheikh Zuwaid and al-Arish in North Sinai. Since July 2013, it has focused almost exclusively on attacking the military, using advanced tactics. It typically relies on a combination of mortars, rocket-propelled grenades (RPGs), and improvised explosive devices (IEDs), which it uses against soldiers, checkpoints and other military targets. These include political and economic infrastructure associated with the army, such as the gas pipeline, military-intelligence buildings and affiliated businesses. In what it described as 'economic warfare' against the state, ABM attacked a tourist bus in Taba, in South Sinai, in February 2014, killing three South Koreans and an Egyptian.

After an attack on 24 October 2014 that killed 33 security personnel, ABM pledged allegiance to ISIS and changed its name to Wilayat Sinai (Sinai Province). Links to ISIS were reported as early as mid-2014, but actual cooperation between the two groups was only confirmed one year later.[3] The decision to join ISIS was designed to take advantage of the well-established notoriety of the group's brand, thereby expanding ABM's influence. Sinai Province has adopted ISIS tactics such as beheadings – particularly of alleged collaborators – arguably inspired by media attention.[4]

As Sinai Province, the group has grown bolder and adopted more advanced tactics. For example, in January 2015, its militants simultaneously attacked a military base and nearby security-affiliated buildings, a military hotel, a police club, a newspaper office and army-patrolled checkpoints, killing more than 40 people. Such attacks aim to dent the credibility of the army, which has repeatedly declared that it has won victories against the insurgents. One year earlier, ABM posted a video of its operatives shooting down a military helicopter using a surface-to-air missile, killing five soldiers. The army initially denied that the attack had taken place.[5] In response to such incidents, the Ministry of Defence has released its own propaganda from soldiers stationed in Sinai, which contains striking parallels with Sinai Province's videos in its inclusion of graphic images of fighting and killings.[6]

Military setbacks in Sinai have forced the government to escalate its operations and deploy additional troops. In January 2015, Sisi established a unified command for counter-terrorism under the leadership of General Osama Askar. Such changes have nevertheless failed to curtail Sinai Province's activity, and people living in the region have reported the continued presence of militant-run checkpoints. The army's presence is largely static, its movements predictable and its capacity for counter-insurgency operations, such as intelligence gathering, limited. In response to recent deployments, a Sinai Province commander stated mockingly: 'don't send reinforcements to Sinai. Send your whole army. It will die in the desert.'[7]

Despite the troop surge, Sinai Province launched in July 2015 a high-profile attack on 11 checkpoints in Sheikh Zuweid, stormed the city and besieged the main police station. Militants roamed the city for the entire day, only withdrawing under heavy aerial bombardment. The group was forced back, but the attack revealed publicly Sinai Province's capacity to outwit, bog down and humiliate the army. It relied predominantly on the shock factor of 'seizing' a city of 60,000 people and holding off heavily armed soldiers, albeit temporarily. In the same month, the group also released photos of an attack with a guided anti-tank missile on a navy vessel off the coast of Rafah.

In addition to undermining the army's credibility, Sinai Province has sought to establish its legitimacy in North Sinai by targeting the symbols and structures of the state. It is attempting to legitimate itself in the eyes of the region's population – and thereby gain popularity and recruits – by exploiting their sense of historic neglect and highlighting the state's history of violence towards them. The group also insists, somewhat disingenuously, that it does not intentionally target civilians, and has apologised for 'errant' attacks on people in the region. It also emphasises its local and even fraternal nature, which its attempts at outreach reflect. In June 2015, the group warned farmers not to use tractors or other heavy agricultural machinery without coordinating with its fighters, to avoid setting off IEDs intended for the security forces.[8] And it posted photos on its Twitter account that showed its fighters distributing compensation to 'victims of the army'.

Sinai Province's emphasis on state injustice can be viewed as an attempt to exploit the strong rifts between Islamists and the military. It has described the judiciary as 'tyrants' and in May 2015 killed three judges, along with 100 other people, hours after a court sentenced Morsi to death. Moreover, before executing a Croatian engineer in August, the group offered to release him in exchange for the release of 'all Muslim women' from jail.

The government's announcement in February 2015 that 73 tribes in Sinai had joined the war against Sinai Province can be interpreted as part of this battle for legitimacy. The statement – disseminated throughout Egyptian media – reflects the government's efforts to reclaim lost legitimacy by showing that it has support on the ground, and that the tide is turning in the war against the *takfiris*. However, there is no evidence of direct confrontation between the tribes and Sinai Province, and the pro-government tribal statements have mostly come from individuals based in Cairo, rather than in Sinai itself.[9] The state has also sought to undermine Sinai Province by depicting it as a foreign affiliate of ISIS, commenting on the presence of foreign fighters in its ranks as inconsistent with its claim to being a local faction.

While the state's approach may eventually weaken Sinai Province, it has also affected the rest of the local population by aggravating political and economic deprivation without offering an alternative narrative. A strictly imposed curfew, under a continuous state of emergency, and indiscriminate crackdowns have paralysed economic activity and killed, maimed or detained civilians. Unemployment has soared and smuggling, which for a long time was the only way for many people to make a living, has become impossible. Even those who support the army question its strategy and behaviour.[10]

The militarisation of the state response is evident in the way the military has re-engineered public spaces for security purposes. Especially controversial was the creation of a 5km buffer zone in the city of Rafah, on the border with the Gaza Strip, which led to the demolition of hundreds of homes and possibly the elimination of the city, with residents offered compensation equivalent to just three months' rent. These civilians described their forced evacuation as a form of collective punishment and 'a declaration of war' against local tribes.[11] Residents of Sheikh Zuweid shared similar concerns after Sinai Province's incursion into the city in July 2015, fearing that the group's operation would be used as a pretence for imposing punitive measures on them. They believe that resettlement has long been part of the government's agenda to secure the strategic area by altering its demographic make-up. This agenda is underpinned by the government's perception of the Bedouins as disloyal and not truly Egyptian.

Another contentious construction project is that for the 7km barrier encircling the city of al-Arish, which reminds residents that their security is secondary to that of the gas pipeline the barrier is designed to protect. This perception is worsened by the fact that, in the eyes of many, this gas is a stolen resource diverted to military-run enterprises in the area, the rest of the country, Jordan and, until recently, Israel.

Government pledges on economic development, which it presented as part of the counter-insurgency campaign, have not materialised, exacerbating the grievances of many locals.[12] Activists jokingly recall that such pledges are forgotten all year round and renewed on Sinai Liberation Day – which has been tellingly referred to as '*eid tahmeesh sina*' (Sinai Marginalisation Day). Regional investment is predominantly funnelled into the lucrative southern tip of the peninsula and its Red Sea tourist resorts. The disparity between North and South Sinai was symbolically reinforced during preparations for the Egyptian Economic Development Conference held in Sharm el-Sheikh in March 2015. Before the conference began, Sisi announced plans to build an industrial zone and a new airport in South Sinai. In contrast, only security-related structures have been built in North Sinai. Reportedly, residents of North Sinai who were present in Sharm el-Sheikh were even forced to leave as a security precaution in the lead-up to another international conference, 'Cape to Cairo', in May.[13]

The portrayal of North Sinai in official statements and state-aligned media amplifies the sense of exclusion, routinely depicting the local population as sponsors or supporters of terrorism, or simply as non-existent, confirming local perceptions that the area lies beyond the imagined geography of the state. The military controls all media in North Sinai, which publish and broadcast intentionally distorted information. In the name of security, the authorities frequently cut telecommunications – including telephone lines and the internet – leading residents to launch a campaign called '*sina kharig al-taghteyya*' (Sinai is out of coverage). The closure of the main bridge into North Sinai from the Nile Valley, al-Salam bridge, other frequent road closures and the establishment of checkpoints contribute to a sense of being under siege. Normal life is a distant memory and, despite allegations of war crimes,[14] the army does not acknowledge civilian casualties caused by its own operations.[15] The increasing popular resentment of the government and the security services reinforces Sinai Province's position, and highlights inequality and the absence of the state.

Beyond Sinai: the spread of violence throughout Egypt

Beyond Sinai, ABM has claimed responsibility for attacks in the Nile Delta region, where a sister organisation has reportedly emerged. It also stated that it was behind an assassination attempt on interior minister Mohamed Ibrahim in Cairo in September 2013 in which his motorcade was attacked with a car bomb in Nasr City. Armed groups operating outside Sinai are loosely affiliated with ABM, although the majority of them are pro-al-Qaeda rather than pro-ISIS. That split is discernible even within ABM, with some factions maintaining allegiance to al-Qaeda leader Ayman al-Zawahiri. Unlike the strong al-Qaeda–ISIS rivalries across the Arab world, alliances in Egypt appear to be more fluid, with reports suggesting that ABM's fighters in Sinai support ISIS, while those in the Nile Delta follow al-Qaeda.

The spread of ABM beyond Sinai and the area northeast of the Suez Canal is part of a wider trend. From mid-2013 onwards, violence began spreading to the rest of Egypt, including the areas of Greater Cairo and Alexandria, and along the western border of the country, where new armed groups are now operating, despite (or perhaps because of) a strong military presence. This escalation is not necessarily linked to shared aims or straightforward collaboration between *takfiris* and Islamists radicalised by the 2013 coup that toppled Morsi. But geographic expansion by the *takfiris* has coincided with Islamists' incremental adoption of violent tactics.

The capacity of militant groups operating in Egypt beyond Sinai is limited compared to their counterparts in North Sinai; however, their attacks have become more frequent. Small-scale bomb attacks in Cairo, which tend to result in minimal casualties, have become widespread – to the extent the popular traffic app Bey2ollak now includes a bomb-alert hashtag.

Such attacks often rely on rudimentary explosives and target parts of the security establishment such as the police, as well as banks, electricity infrastructure, water towers, shopping malls, mobile-phone companies, restaurants, railways, the Cairo metro and the airport. Their aim is to discredit the state and its claim to maintaining order and control. The targets are often related to a specific event, such as the anniversary of the uprising, or the economic conference that took place in Sharm el-Sheikh in March, which was meant to strengthen Sisi's legitimacy.

Ajnad Misr (Soldiers of Egypt) has claimed responsibility for many of the attacks that have taken place in Greater Cairo.

The group officially announced its formation in January 2014 following a string of attacks that began in November 2013. It has subsequently taken responsibility for at least 20 attacks, which have killed around 20 people, mostly police officers. ABM has described Ajnad Misr as 'our brothers', but the extent of relations between the two groups is not entirely clear.[16] Although both groups target state infrastructure, Ajnad Misr focuses on structures and figures related to the interior ministry, such as police stations and officers, rather than the military, possibly due to a lack of capability. This comparatively low capacity is also evident in Ajnad Misr's use of tactics and weaponry less advanced than those of ABM – most of its attacks have involved basic IEDs.

While little is known about Ajnad Misr's structure, the killing of its leader, a shadowy figure known as Hammam Attiyah, by security forces in April 2015 placed the group firmly within al-Qaeda's orbit, and prompted condolences from al-Qaeda in the Arabian Peninsula and al-Qaeda in the Islamic Maghreb.[17] Egyptian security sources have suggested that Attiyah had been involved in militant activity in Sinai and left to establish Ajnad Misr in Cairo, possibly with the aim of bringing the violence closer to the capital.[18]

Ajnad Misr's appeal and operational model are based on motivating supporters to launch lone-wolf attacks, rather than launching advanced, organised attacks.[19] Like ABM, Ajnad Misr claims not to target civilians, insisting that its main target is the security forces. The group draws on a revolutionary narrative of resisting a violent and illegitimate regime, singling out crimes committed by security forces and police officers. It seeks to win over the Egyptian people, claiming that it does not harm innocent bystanders or those who disagree with its agenda. On the first anniversary of the 30 June demonstrations that led to Morsi's ousting, Ajnad Misr warned people to stay away from the presidential palace in Ittihadiya, where it had planted several bombs, until it apparently aborted the mission over fears of inflicting civilian casualties.[20]

Because Ajnad Misr is an unintended product of the post-coup order, the government has conveniently linked it to the Brotherhood. Equating the Brotherhood's ideology with 'takfirism' aims to delegitimise the organisation, undermine its appeal and treat it as a terrorist group; the approach also works to ensure that the Brotherhood can no longer function as a credible opposition movement.

Security officials have described Ajnad Misr as the armed wing of the Brotherhood, even suggesting that the militants have direct links to the Brotherhood leadership, in particular Deputy-General Guide Khairat al-Shater, although there is scant evidence of an ordered relationship. While ABM previously appealed to the Brotherhood to abandon its 'humiliating nonviolence',[21] there is no evidence that pro-Morsi supporters have allied with takfiri groups.

Nevertheless, alienated citizens affiliated with the Brotherhood's Popular Resistance Movements have begun to strike back with crude attacks,[22] such as throwing Molotov cocktails at police stations. Members of this group include radicalised factions of the National Alliance to Support Legitimacy, an organisation that supports Morsi and was formed after his ouster. For the first time since the movement officially rejected violence, during the 1970s and 1980s, members of the Brotherhood – and youth groups in particular – are increasingly calling for violence and even, in extreme cases, a reactivation of its paramilitary forces.[23]

The highest-profile attack that the Popular Resistance Movements have claimed responsibility for is the assassination of chief prosecutor Hisham Barakat on 29 June 2015. If this claim is true, the murder suggests not only a qualitative escalation against the state, but also a significant expansion of the group's capacity. Barakat sentenced hundreds of Brotherhood members to death, including Morsi himself. Shortly after Barakat's assassination, the army killed 13 figures affiliated with the Brotherhood, including a former legislator, drawing the most explicit call to arms yet by the Brotherhood's leadership.[24] Violence in this case is depicted as a reaction: according to the Brotherhood, the state declared war on the movement, rather than vice versa.

This radicalisation and splintering of factions within the Brotherhood may be attributed to the government's heavy-handed security response, its dismissal of any serious reconciliation efforts and its declared desire to uproot the movement politically and socially. While the military has publicly eulogised the deaths of members of the security forces in official statements and on television, killings of Brotherhood supporters often go unmentioned and without condemnation, feeding resentment and further radicalisation. At the same time, there is a tacit understanding that members of the security forces who kill Brotherhood-affiliated 'terrorists' will not be held accountable.[25]

The Libyan front: spillover and intervention

Confronting threats has also prompted the security establishment to operate beyond Egypt's borders, most notably in Libya. Libya has been in turmoil since 2011 as multiple armed militias vie for control of the state, posing security challenges for Egypt. As Libya became awash with weapons after 2011, the western border saw more smuggling and trafficking. Security agencies trace the flood of light and heavy weapons into the Egyptian market back to Libya's instability. The growing availability of such weapons has significantly driven down their price: the price of shoulder-fired anti-aircraft missiles, for example, has dropped by more than half.[26] Authorities have attempted to clamp down on this trade, and regularly seize automatic rifles and ammunition, RPGs, *Grad* rockets and anti-aircraft guns. In addition to deploying additional troops to secure the border with Libya, Egyptian officials have approached the US to purchase mobile-surveillance sensor systems.

Nevertheless, there have not been cross-border attacks from Libya as of mid-2015, and militant activity along the western border is significantly lower than in places such as Sinai, largely because Libyan factions are focused inwards and Egyptian allies operate on Libya's eastern border. A notable exception was an attack against 21 border guards in the New Valley region in July 2014. ABM claimed responsibility for the incident, despite not being known to have a presence in the region, and the simultaneous, coordinated attacks bore a resemblance to the group's modus operandi.

So far, the military has intervened twice to contain the spillover from the Libyan civil war – once covertly and once overtly. The first intervention entailed joint Egyptian–Emirati aerial raids designed to slow down the imminent takeover of Tripoli airport by Islamist militias in August 2014, which was revealed by US officials but denied by the Egyptian military and foreign ministry.[27] The second attack, which took place in February 2015, followed the beheading of 21 Egyptian Coptic Christian hostages by a pro-ISIS group in Sirte. The Egyptian air force responded by attacking targets in Derna and Sirte, which reportedly included positions, training camps and weapons-storage facilities.

In the second attack, the government sought to divert attention away from the embarrassment of the hostage crisis by emphasising that it was avenging Egypt's Christians, whose kidnapping had been preceded by numerous attacks on, and abductions of, Egyptian migrant workers in Libya. The airstrikes showed Sisi's ostensible support for Egypt's minority Christian population, many of whom were particularly concerned about the rise of jihadism, and served to illustrate the state's commitment to fighting Islamism, which it portrayed as a region-wide threat.

For Sisi, the raid in Libya accomplished more than just scoring domestic points: it also demonstrated how he envisioned Egypt's role in the post-2013 order – using its strong military to protect regional stability – and positioned Egypt in the informal anti-ISIS coalition. The government has resisted dialogue with the Islamist-dominated Tripoli government, instead supporting the ostensibly anti-Islamist government in Tobruk. Egypt has pressed the UN to sanction further military intervention in Libya and impose a naval blockade against the Tripoli government.

These two instances of military intervention in Libya also reveal operational collaboration between the Sisi government and the forces of General Khalifa Haftar, a self-styled Libyan nationalist commander aligned with the Tobruk government. Seeking to emulate Sisi, Haftar is leading his own war on terror in Libya in pursuit of stability, and he has clashed with Islamist groups and Salafist jihadists. Many Egyptians and international observers speculate that Sisi, in working with Haftar, wishes to install a like-minded figure in Libya to cooperate on security threats. Some reports suggest that the Sisi government has delivered weaponry to Haftar's forces,[28] but others say that it has only provided training and technical assistance.[29] Although Egypt's involvement risks embroiling the country in the Libyan civil war, it achieves Sisi's goals of regional and international legitimacy, and broadening the fight against Islamism in all its forms.

The Sisi strategy and the militarisation project

The array of security threats facing Egypt are grave and have already affected everyday life. However, the government's response has only contributed to insecurity and has long-term implications for the country's political trajectory. Security threats have been used to pursue a state-building project that normalises violence and enshrines the military as the guardian of the nation. This allows the army to control national politics and place itself above criticism, becoming inaccessible and unaccountable to citizens. Due to security threats, the army does not have to devolve power to other bodies or actors to govern or provide necessary public services. (In one leaked audio recording of Sisi's conversations with top generals, they are heard laughing at the dysfunction of civilian bodies, namely the health ministry.[30]) External developments, such as growing regional instability and the rise of Islamist militancy, have fed into this militarisation of domestic and security politics. The Sisi government treats *takfiri* groups aligned with ISIS and al-Qaeda, pro-Brotherhood factions and Libyan Islamist militias as a unified and coherent manifestation of Islamist ideology. However, the government has chosen to exclude from this categorisation organised Salafist groups that allied with it in the aftermath of the coup against Morsi. Within this pragmatic alliance, the Salafist parties emerged from the coup intact, but reconciled themselves to playing a limited role in politics.[31] This suggests that the threats associated with Islamist ideology pertain less to the ideology per se than to groups' ability to challenge the state's legitimacy. By framing these threats as similar, connected and reinforcing, the military has deemed these Islamists a threat to national security and, accordingly, pushed for offensive action. This move is also in line with Egypt's desire to establish a regional anti-Islamist alliance.

In particular, the government has accused the Brotherhood of orchestrating, or at least nurturing, the violence in Sinai, linking the rise of *takfiri* groups to Morsi's one-year rule and presenting Hamas as an intermediary between the Brotherhood and tribal and Islamist groups in North Sinai involved in smuggling and other criminal activities. Some evidence points to the significant role that former Egyptian army officers have played in the insurgency in Sinai.[32] In July 2015, a former special-forces officer who had defected to the *takfiris*, Hisham al-Ashmawi, announced the establishment of a new al-Qaeda-linked armed group, al-Mourabitoun. Egyptian security sources have implicated him in several attacks, including the assassination attempt on Ibrahim in 2013, and allege that there has been collaboration between Ashmawi and Sinai Province.[33] Ashmawi has claimed that he was reacting to the 'imposition of the most severe types of torture and torment against Muslims' under 'the new pharaoh'.[34]

Meanwhile, the undeniably growing links between armed groups in North Sinai and ISIS have allowed the government to frame military operations in North Sinai as part of a counter-terrorism effort against the expansion of the transnational group, disregarding local factors that underpin the *takfiri* threat in Egypt. This has enabled Sisi to present his heavy-handed approach as part of the wider effort against ISIS, and to seek a role for Egypt within the international coalition to legitimise his approach – requesting weapons and other military support from allies to counter ISIS-linked militants in Egypt, and calling for a military intervention in Libya to confront ISIS there.[35]

In particular, Sisi has tried to convince US Secretary of State John Kerry that the international coalition against ISIS should take action against 'all Islamist extremists', a category in which he includes the Brotherhood and other political opponents.[36] He reiterated this call during a speech he made before the UN General Assembly in 2015. Presenting his actions against the Brotherhood as part of the fight against ISIS is an attempt to gain tacit legitimacy (and perhaps even assistance) for crackdowns against the Brotherhood and other political opponents. At the same time, the way the government has dealt with external crises, notably the situation in Libya, reflects Egypt's desire to be a credible, leading partner in regional security coalitions spearheaded by its primary allies, Saudi Arabia and the UAE.

The chaotic regional atmosphere has given the Egyptian military considerable leeway in relations with international actors and critics of its counter-terrorism operations. By painting a broad picture of Islamist threats and refusing to make any distinction between armed groups and those seeking to participate in the political process, militarisation may be pushing moderates to adopt the extremists' tactics.

Conclusion

Two years after its launch, the self-proclaimed war on terror has expanded in scope, reach and intensity. Militants, political opponents, dissidents and activists have all been lumped together as terrorists. The government's hyper-nationalistic rhetoric labels them all as outcasts who are seeking to destabilise the state. Terrorism laws have permitted further restrictions on freedoms: Sisi has passed a series of presidential decrees that culminated in the controversial decision in October 2014 to place all public infrastructure under the jurisdiction and protection of the military. This move has led to hundreds of civilians being tried in military courts.[37] Many suspects have been detained in unofficial military prisons.[38]

Another counter-terrorism law, passed in August 2015, criminalised reporting that contradicted the state's official account in any terrorism-related context – yet another indication of the move towards a monopoly on information. The legislation also granted security forces additional immunity from prosecution, created special courts to expedite trials for those accused of crimes that fall into the category of terrorism, and granted prosecutors additional powers to carry out surveillance and detention. In June 2014, the interior ministry contracted private firms to monitor the online activity of Egyptians and thereby track security threats.[39] These moves are part of a wider trend that equates even the slightest form of dissent with slander and a lack of patriotism.

The way in which Sisi rose to power in 2013 and his credentials as a military strongman are relevant to the current design of Egypt's policy responses – and this was undoubtedly part of his appeal to an Egyptian public exhausted and unnerved by two and a half years of a chaotic transition. Yet this unprecedented deployment of force may well exacerbate rather than resolve the sources of instability, and prove to be counterproductive to Sisi's proclaimed goal of restoring order.

Nonetheless, the spread of militant violence – in Egypt and throughout the region – serves Sisi's short-term political goals. The rise of ISIS, and especially its affiliate in Sinai, have increased popular support for the military's counter-terrorism operations.[40] Having watched the unravelling of Syria, Iraq and Libya, many Egyptians are willing to accept the return of the security state and its associated costs. Internationally, the military has presented itself as a key player in regional anti-Islamist alliances, facilitating Egypt's regional and international reintegration.

While the Egyptian government has long complained of its Western allies' inability to fully grasp the threats it faces, it now benefits from international acquiescence to its war on terror. Egypt faced little condemnation when it intervened in Libya without an international mandate. On the contrary, the response has been accepted as necessary for defence and deterrence.

These events suggest why the US resumed military aid to Egypt after suspending it in 2013. Having delivered a first shipment of *Apache* helicopters to Egypt at the end of 2014, the US proceeded in March 2015 to release military aid worth US$1.5 billion, which had been frozen in the wake of the post-coup violence, followed by F-16 fighter jets and tank turrets in July. Other countries, including France and Russia, have scrambled to sign arms deals with Egypt.

Under Sisi, military force coupled with an ultra-nationalist, exclusionary narrative has become the principal state response to security challenges, at the expense of more nuanced political and socio-economic approaches. This wilful ignorance of Egypt's recent history is likely to feed the insurgency that plagues the country for the foreseeable future.

Notes

1 The term *takfiri* refers to groups that accuse other Muslims of *kufr* (apostasy). *Takfiri* groups have historically operated in Sinai and elsewhere in Egypt, and have launched high-profile attacks against tourists. The Mubarak government put down an insurgency by *takfiri* groups in the 1990s.

2 Locals have often disputed the government's definition of 'militants', saying that many of the people killed, injured and arrested were civilians. See reports by Sinai-based journalists, such as Mona El Zamlout and Mohannad Sabry.

3 'Exclusive: Islamic State Guides Egyptian Militants, Expanding its Influence', Reuters, 5 September 2014, http://www.reuters.com/article/2014/09/05/us-egypt-islamicstate-idUSKBN0H018F20140905.

4 Data from the Armed Conflict Database suggests that ABM/Sinai Province has beheaded at least 27 people. See Armed Conflict Database, https://acd.iiss.org/en/conflicts/egypt-sinai-279c.

5 See 'Ansar Bayt al-Maqdis Shoots Down Egyptian Army Helicopter in Sinai', https://www.youtube.com/watch?v=QWztP6rDges.

6 '*Risyalat al-jaysh al-masri min sina*', https://www.youtube.com/watch?v=u-nD-HbLcfg. For analysis of the video and a comparison with Ansar Bayt al-Maqdis's propaganda, see Laura Gribbon, 'You Show Me Yours and I'll Show You Mine', *Mada Masr*, 22 December 2014, http://www.madamasr.com/sections/politics/you-show-me-yours-and-ill-show-you-mine.

7 Omar Ashour, 'Sinai's Enduring Insurgency', Al-Jazeera, 20 April 2015, http://www.aljazeera.com/indepth/opinion/2015/04/sinai-enduring-insurgency-150419080316130.html.

8 'Sinai Province Warns Bedouins Against Using Tractors to Avoid IEDs', *Cairo Post*, 14 June 2015, http://www.thecairopost.com/news/155429/news/sinai-province-warns-bedouins-against-using-tractors-to-avoid-ieds.

9 Mokhar Awad and Mostafa Abdou, 'A New Sinai Battle? Bedouin Tribes and Egypt's ISIS Affiliate', Atlantic Council, 14 May 2015, http://www.atlanticcouncil.org/blogs/egyptsource/a-new-sinai-battle-bedouin-tribes-and-egypt-s-isis-affiliate.

10 An activist from Rafah was reported to have said: 'we were extremely delighted that the army had entered Sinai for the first time after the withdrawal of the police ... The residents unanimously agreed on the need to support the army and to turn a new page ... So we were surprised that in its crackdowns over the past two years, the army did not differentiate between the extremists and us.' 'In Sinai Residents Feel Betrayed by Egyptian Media', translated by Joelle el-Khory, *Al-Monitor*, 26 February 2015, http://www.al-monitor.com/pulse/originals/2015/02/egypt-media-biased-sinai-residents-terrorism-army.html.

11 Mohammed Salem, 'Reshaping the City of Rafah in Sinai: Expulsion Threatens War with the Tribes', *Al Akhbar English*, 5 November 2014, http://english.al-akhbar.com/node/22347.

12 'Sinai Ignored in Egypt Development Plans', *Al-Monitor*, 1 May 2014, http://www.al-monitor.com/pulse/originals/2014/04/sinai-egypt-residents-anger-empty-government-promises.html.

13 Hamada al-Shawadfi, '*Foda yutalib bi-tarheel 'adad min abnaa Sina al-mutasallilleen ila Sharm el-Sheikh*', *Shorouk News*, 15 May 2015, http://www.shorouknews.com/news/view.aspx?cdate=15052015&id=fa0c2723-3643-46a3-9c77-66c9bac1bd30.

14 See report by the Egyptian Observatory for Rights and Freedoms, '*Hisad al-Tawareq: jara'im sittet ushhur fi halit al-tawariq fi sina*', 25 April 2014, available at http://www.slideshare.net/ssuserd93812/1-3991847.

15 Regular updates by the military's spokesperson do not include civilian casualties, unless they are caused by armed groups. See https://www.facebook.com/Egy.Army.Spox?fref=nf.

16 See the Tahrir Institute for Middle East Policy's description of Ajnad Misr, available at http://timep.org/esw/profiles/terror-groups/ajnad-misr/.

17 Thomas Joscelyn, 'Al Qaeda Branches Eulogize Slain Egyptian Jihadist', *Long War Journal*, 13 April 2015, http://www.longwarjournal.org/archives/2015/04/al-qaeda-branches-eulogize-slain-egyptian-jihadist.php.

18 'Founder of Islamist Militant Group Ajnad Misr Killed: Police Spokesman', Ahram Online, 5 April 2015, http://english.ahram.org.eg/NewsContent/1/64/126984/Egypt/Politics-/Founder-of-Islamist-militant-group-Ajnad-Misr-kill.aspx.

19 Wissam Matta, '*Ajnad Misr: dhi'ab mutawahida nashi'a*', *Assafir*, 2 July 2014, http://assafir.com/Article/1/359009.

20 Maggie Fick, 'Police Officers Killed in Bomb Blasts Near Cairo', Reuters, 30 June 2014, http://www.reuters.com/article/2014/06/30/us-egypt-blast-idUSKBN0F50Q720140630.

21 'Egypt's Ansar Beit al-Maqdis Pledges Allegiance to ISIS', Al Akhbar English, 10 November 2014, http://english.al-akhbar.com/node/22399.

22 See the Twitter pages linked to the Popular Resistance Movements, such as https://twitter.com/moqawamaegy.

23 Mokhtar Awad and Nathan J. Brown, 'Mutual Escalation in Egypt', Washington Post, 9 February 2015, http://www.washingtonpost.com/blogs/monkey-cage/wp/2015/02/09/mutual-escalation-in-egypt/.

24 'The Latest: Muslim Brotherhood Calls for Egypt "Rebellion"', Associated Press, 1 July 2015, http://bigstory.ap.org/article/e77c284bd6ec4b3dbcf1e7b9bcdd084d/latest-militant-attacks-egypts-sinai-kill-30-troops.

25 An obvious example of this is the massacre at Rabaa al-Adawiya. Another is the case of 37 prisoners who suffocated to death in the back of a police van. See Priyanka Motaparthy, 'The Unknown Man and the Deaths at Abu Zaabal', New Yorker, 3 April 2015, http://www.newyorker.com/news/news-desk/the-unknown-man-and-the-deaths-at-abu-zaabal.

26 Sources say it dropped from US$10,000 to US$4,000. See Nicholas Pelham, 'Sinai: The Buffer Erodes', Chatham House, September 2012, available at http://www.chathamhouse.org/sites/files/chathamhouse/public/Research/Middle%20East/pr0912pelham.pdf.

27 Patrick Kingsley, Chris Stephen and Dan Roberts, 'UAE and Egypt Behind Bombing Raids Against Libyan Militias, Say US Officials', Guardian, 29 August 2014, http://www.theguardian.com/world/2014/aug/26/united-arab-emirates-bombing-raids-libyan-militias.

28 'Audio Leaks "Show UAE and Egypt Shipped Arms to Haftar"', Al-Jazeera, 22 May 2015, http://www.aljazeera.com/news/2015/05/audio-leaks-show-uae-egypt-shipped-arms-haftar-150522004256136.html.

29 Ayah Aman, 'Egypt Looks to Roll Back Islamist Militias in Libya', Al-Monitor, translated by Pascale Menassa, 12 December 2014, http://www.al-monitor.com/pulse/originals/2014/12/egypt-coordinate-libya-defeat-islamists.html.

30 David Kirkpatrick, 'Leaks Gain Credibility and Potential to Embarrass Egypt's Leaders', New York Times, 12 May 2015, http://www.nytimes.com/2015/05/13/world/middleeast/leaks-gain-credibility-and-potential-to-embarrass-egypts-leaders.html?_r=0.

31 A well-known example is al-Nour Party. See Jonathan Brown, 'The Rise and Fall of the Salafi al-Nour Party in Egypt', Jadaliyya, 14 November 2013, available at http://www.jadaliyya.com/pages/index/15113/the-rise-and-fall-of-the-salafi-al-nour-party-in-e.

32 Yara Bayoumy, 'Insight – in Egypt, Ex-Military Men Fire Up Islamist Insurgency', Reuters, 7 April 2015, http://uk.reuters.

com/article/2015/04/07/uk-egypt-militants-military-insight-idUKKBN0MY1PP20150407.

33 Thomas Joscelyn and Caleb Weiss, 'Former Egyptian Special Forces Officer Leads Al Murabitoon', *Long War Journal*, 23 July 2015, http://www.longwarjournal.org/archives/2015/07/former-egyptian-special-forces-officer-leads-al-murabitoon.php.

34 See *'Dhabet al-sa'qah al-misriyya al-munshaq Hisham al-Ashmawi, emir jama'at al-mourabitoun fi sina'*, YouTube, https://www.youtube.com/watch?v=nuiFKEU9rXM.

35 Ian Black, 'Egyptian President Calls for United Nations Military Action in Libya', *Guardian*, 17 February 2015, http://www.theguardian.com/world/2015/feb/17/egyptian-president-sisi-libya-islamic-state-lukewarm-europe-coptic-un.

36 Jason Szep and Shadi Bushra, 'Egypt Says Global Action Needed to Counter Islamic State', Reuters, 13 September 2014, http://www.reuters.com/article/2014/09/13/us-egypt-islamicstate-idUSKBN0H80ER20140913.

37 'Egypt: Surge of Military Trials', Human Rights Watch, 18 December 2014, https://www.hrw.org/news/2014/12/18/egypt-surge-military-trials.

38 Tom Stevenson, 'Sisi's Way', *London Review of Books*, vol. 37, no. 14, 19 February 2015, available at http://www.lrb.co.uk/v37/n04/tom-stevenson/sisis-way.

39 'Egypt, Citing Security, Wants Foreign Companies to Help Monitor Social Media', *Reuters*, 2 June 2014, http://www.reuters.com/article/2014/06/02/us-egypt-media-idUSKBN0ED1EX20140602.

40 Gregory Aftandilian, 'Assessing Egyptian Public Support for Security Crackdowns in the Sinai', Strategic Studies Institute and US Army War College Press, February 2015, available at http://www.strategicstudiesinstitute.army.mil/pdffiles/PUB1249.pdf.

CHAPTER NINE

The Egyptian economy

Mohamed El Dahshan

Two out of the three demands of the slogan of Egypt's 2011 revolution – 'Bread, freedom, and social justice' – were fundamentally economic. Although triggered by political events, the revolution reflected the collapse of the implicit social contract between the state and its citizens, in which people had traded political rights for a basic livelihood. The government relied on economic devices, including subsidised energy, transportation and essential foodstuffs, to walk this tightrope. Its inflated public sector, employing 5.5 million civil servants by the end 2010, was another aspect of this rentierist strategy. During the final days of the revolution and afterwards, workers in large state-owned factories participated in around 60 strikes. The targeted companies – strategic workplaces such as the Cairo Public Transport Authority, Egyptian State Railways, subsidiary companies of the Suez Canal Authority and the state's electricity company – and the coordination among tens of thousands of workers suggested the effective collapse of this contract.[1] Despite an official growth rate surpassing 6% in the five years leading up to the revolution, the liberalisation agenda that the government had pursued

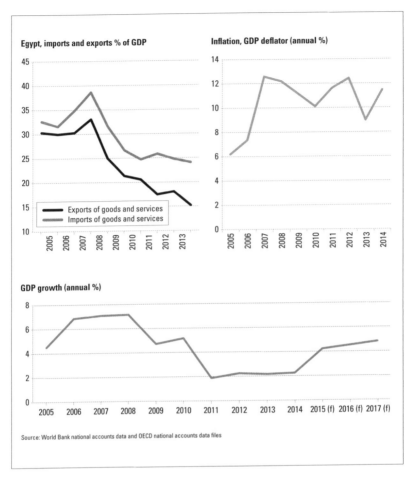

Figure 1. **Imports/exports; inflation and GDP growth**

under Hosni Mubarak in the 2000s had caused distress among the population. Similar to other comparable cases, economic liberalisation in Egypt generated growth that barely 'trickled down'. At the same time, the rapid pace of change, cronyism and scant attention to social justice generated significant discontent. Rampant inflation and currency devaluation meant that already low wages could not meet basic needs. Following the privatisation of state-owned enterprises, jobs became increasingly scarce, with rising youth unemployment. Objections to the economic situation preceded the revolution; from 2006 onwards, there were regular strikes, such as the famous general strike in April 2008. Keeping in mind structural challenges, including food and energy short-ages, this chapter will discuss and evaluate the economic platforms of successive actors since the 2011 uprising. Egypt's economic story since the uprising has been one of destruc-tive inaction, but this has just begun to change. The economic vision of President Abdel Fattah Al-Sisi, dubbed 'Sisinomics', is a radical departure from the slow and cautious process of economic change that characterised the 2011–13 period. Sisi has combined a business-friendly approach, as showcased in the economic conference held in Sharm el-Sheikh in March 2015, with an enduring role for the military as an engine of development, notably through its involvement in ambitious projects such as the 'New Suez Canal'. However, Sisinomics carries many risks; despite the hype, it has overlooked essential demands, such as social justice and economic inclu-siveness.

Egypt under the SCAF: short-term calculations

No time seems as auspicious for economic reform as the after-math of a popular revolution: the sudden disruption suggests that the public may be most willing to accept and withstand changes. Yet the Supreme Council of the Armed Forces (SCAF), which governed the country following Mubarak's resignation in 2011, refused to undertake necessary reforms to strengthen the economy. Instead, it largely chose to continue with the status quo that had brought about the revolution in the first place, the only changes being occasional temporary meas-ures. The first act of the new government, for example, was to approve 450,000 permanent contracts to temporary workers in the already bloated public sector, along with a 15% increase in salaries and a boost in pensions.[2]

Another 'quick fix' addressed the swift decline in foreign reserves: the SCAF 'donated' in December 2011 US$1 billion to efforts designed to replenish the central bank's declining foreign-currency reserves and keep the currency from depreciating, which would have potentially fuelled unrest. Similarly, subsidies for fuel and food were raised by 75% from around US$15bn to around US$26bn.[3] These moves amounted to a political manoeuvre that did not account for the economy's fundamental ills. They were a conscious decision not to engage with economic problems, driven by the SCAF's awareness of its limited political capital. The SCAF chose not to rock the boat, even if this meant further aggravating the country's economic problems in the longer term.

The SCAF's engagement with the IMF, another case of a deliberately missed opportunity, illustrates its deliberate neglect of the economy. During the post-revolutionary euphoria of the few months following the removal of Mubarak, an IMF team flew to Cairo and offered the government a package worth US$3bn. The package enables the government to set its own benchmarks for progress, in stark contrast to the IMF's usual practice of making loans conditional on reforms that follow a strict schedule. The offer was something of a blank cheque. Discussions with finance minister Samir Radwan were positive; Radwan went as far as to announce publicly that negotiations had concluded with an agreement to be 'signed any minute now'.[4] But it never was. The government stalled and ultimately shelved the deal, citing 'popular distrust'. Despite the favourable terms of the stand-by loan, with interest slightly above 1%, the media attacked the deal.[5] The negative coverage was surprising because the public usually showed little interest in such matters, leading to suggestions that the government had orchestrated it in a bid to earn populist points – once again, at the expense of the welfare of the people.

Egypt under the Muslim Brotherhood: the wrong experiments at the worst possible time

President Muhammad Morsi's one-year rule came with many strings attached. Coming to power in the June 2012 presidential elections with a 51.73% majority, with probably half of the electorate voting against the opposite candidate, he took office with a shaky mandate. The economic uncertainty that the revolution had caused only made things worse. Such uncertainty was exacerbated by the Brotherhood's incoherent economic approach, which was characterised by two competing visions.[6] One strongly favoured the free market, which powerful business interests in the movement advanced; the other was inherently redistributive and top-down, motivated by the Brotherhood's long-standing tradition of charity and financial aid. This fundamental divergence affected the government's development policy; in fact, the Brotherhood's political arm, the Freedom and Justice Party (FJP), listed its poverty-alleviation strategy under social justice rather than economic development. The only economic vision that Morsi articulated was a manifesto developed by Brotherhood financier Khairat al-Shater. This 'Renaissance Project'[7] was a 20-year plan that promised growth rates of up to 7% within five years, but contained no clear explanation of how to achieve this. It lacked short-term measures and quick wins, which were necessary to redress the economy and alleviate popular anxiety. The plan never seemed to gain much support, and after a few months it was quietly withdrawn from the president's speech. One of Morsi's early mistakes was to give free rein to the powerful businesspeople who supported the Brotherhood, facilitating their takeover of private interests. This essentially replicated the crony capitalism of the Mubarak era, which had inflamed public anger towards his regime. The creation of the Egyptian Business Development Association (EBDA) in July 2012 was a case in point.[8] Headed by another Brotherhood financier, Hassan Malek, the EBDA acted as a new parallel business association.[9] Although it initially presented itself as free from the cronyism that had characterised the uncomfortably close government–business ties in the pre-revolutionary era, it quickly evolved to replicate these same ties. Business delegations composed largely of EBDA members accompanied Morsi on trips abroad, as did Mubarak-connected tycoons.[10] Morsi was careful not to upset military interests, acutely aware that he did not have support in its ranks. He went as far as to submit a draft constitution in December 2012 that gave the military immunity from prosecution by civilian anti-corruption authorities. The army was nonetheless nervous, insisting 'on having a role and veto power [in the country's economic affairs], suggesting that it felt challenged by the Morsi presidency', in the words of analyst Ziyad Sayegh.[11] The economic-policy rift with the army undoubtedly hastened Morsi's ouster.

During his year in office, the Egyptian pound, overvalued since the revolution, lost 15% of its value against the US dollar. With dwindling foreign-currency reserves and no prospect of replenishing them, the central bank imposed limitations on foreign-currency withdrawals and began auctioning dollars, allowing the value of the pound to slide and leading to the inflation of the prices of imported goods and fuel. This measure was seen as delayed damage control, possibly coming too late, while increasing the pain of austerity for the poorest Egyptians.

In addition to Morsi's political blunders, a growing energy crisis contributed in no small part to his demise. Inheriting regular shortages of fuel, the government initially tried to clamp down on profiteering and the black market in subsidised gas and butane canisters, but with little success, particularly outside of Cairo.[12] As summer approached and consumption increased, stop-gap measures, such as importing emergency

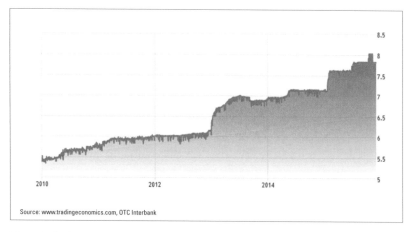

Source: www.tradingeconomics.com, OTC Interbank

Figure 2. **Exchange rate: Egyptian pound/US$, 2010–15**

gas supplies from Qatar under a swap deal and eased terms for Libyan oil purchases,[13] were insufficient to meet demand. Power cuts lasted up to 12 hours per day in some parts of the country, and queues at fuel stations became an ordeal that lasted at least an hour, with motorists regularly pushing their dry cars up the queue.[14] The energy crisis, combined with the replication of government–business ties and a weak economic-development policy, contributed to popular discontent, culminating in the demonstrations in June 2013 that led to Morsi's ousting. In his last speech before he was ousted, Morsi dwelled on the fuel crisis, particularly the long lines at fuel stations and the selling of subsidised fuel on the black market.

The rise of Sisinomics

In the first few months after Morsi's removal from office, there was little appetite for discussions on economic policy. Sisi's ascent was dominated by bloody disputes with the Brotherhood and its supporters, and, having received a stimulus package worth US$12bn from Saudi Arabia, the United Arab Emirates and Kuwait, he could afford to ignore economic policy temporarily. The much-needed economic assistance was a strong indication of support for Sisi and a way to shore up his legitimacy and viability. It also emboldened the government to suspend negotiations with the IMF, with Minister of Planning Ashraf al-Araby declaring that it was 'not appropriate to have a new round of negotiations with the IMF until Egypt [regained] political stability'.[15]

As he began campaigning for the May 2014 presidential election, Sisi's economic message was bleak. His speeches were peppered with references to economic austerity, suggesting that people should 'give up a month's salary' and that young people 'need to give and not expect to take anything now'.[16] This was apparently of little importance to the public, who appeared to overwhelmingly back him. Such popular support, unseen since the revolution – and perhaps long before – would give Sisi free rein in policymaking, economic or otherwise, without the need to consider political calculations and concerns over unpopular measures.

It was telling that he released his formal economic programme only a week before the election, and that it only contained vague plans at best. The plan's key point was its proposed investment policy, which promised to reform legislation and establish an 'investment map' that would guide the development of 26 cities and tourist centres across 21 governorates, as well the Suez Canal Development Plan.[17] Popularly known as the New Suez Canal, the mega-project entailed the construction of a second corridor running parallel to the original canal, allowing for fast shipping in both directions and reducing transit times from 18 to 11 hours. The hope is that the project will double the amount of traffic transiting the canal and increase revenue from US$5.4bn in 2014 to US$13.5bn in 2023. The undertaking also involved the establishment of a development zone between the two waterways, which the investment minister suggested would eventually come to make up 30–35%

of the national economy.[18] The project is to be complemented by the creation of the Suez Canal Zone (SCZone), which would include 100 square kilometres of port and logistics areas, and more than 40 square kilometres of land for industrial and real-estate development, designed to establish a global logistics hub and industrial-processing centre.[19]

The project has come to typify Sisinomics and the shift from the modest economic reforms that Sisi's predecessors had enacted since the revolution. The swift process of, and fundraising efforts for, the project indicates its importance. The digging of the new waterway was completed in just one year and the canal opened for use in August 2015. Meanwhile, fundraising for the project relied heavily on selling tax-free, high-return bonds of denominations as small as US$1.4. The certificates reached the collection target of US$8.5bn within days of their release, testament to the widespread public support for Sisi and his policies – despite the absence of feasibility studies. Individuals purchased the vast majority of the certificates (82%), and institutions the rest; 42% of the money collected came from outside of the banking sector, essentially from household savings.[20]

Very soon, however, experts began to express scepticism about the project, wary that the government may have been overly optimistic – a quality that would become a key characteristic of Sisinomics. They believe the government was overconfident in its projections, casting doubt over estimates about the project's returns, given that doubling traffic depended not only on the canal's capacity but also on global traffic.[21] The long-term impact of the project and the success of the SCZone are uncertain.

2015: the Egypt Economic Development Conference and future plans

It was only in 2015, half a year into his presidency and more than 18 months since he had assumed power, that Sisi's economic ideas began to coalesce into a semblance of a formulated policy – to the great relief of all economic actors and observers. However, this policy was never as well articulated by the president and his top ministers to domestic audiences as it was to foreign ones, in a bid to sway foreign investors and trade partners. Sisi presented a near-complete economic policy during his first appearance before the annual World Economic Forum meeting in Davos in January 2015. In an address titled 'Egypt in the World', he announced a structured plan to reduce the budget deficit, gradually discarding energy subsidies and reforming the tax system to increase revenue, while improving the investment climate, with the goal of achieving a growth rate of 7% and reducing unemployment to 10% by the year 2020.[22] This echoed the most visible and largely well-received reform to date: the overnight reduction of energy subsidies by one-third in July 2014 – a move that successive previous governments had shied away from.[23] The annual-subsidy bill was slashed from more than 20% to 13% of government spending,[24] leading diesel prices to soar by 64%, while the price of low-value Octane 80 gas rose by 78% and that of liquefied natural gas by 175%. Prices were also raised in the electricity sector, which the government intends to partially privatise. While there are still concerns about the impact of these policies on the poorest Egyptians, which has not been studied or addressed, subsidy reduction has been hailed by the IMF as an important measure to reduce the deficit and has boosted investor confidence.[25] Additional reforms – enacted by presidential decree, in the absence of a legislature – have sought to boost private and international investment. Investors have welcomed these moves, and economists share a generally optimistic outlook on the economy, although the real impact of the reforms is a longer-term matter. The bid to woo investors climaxed in March 2015 with the Egypt Economic Development Conference (EEDC), a donor-cum-investment conference held in Sharm el-Sheikh. The government touted it as the foundation of the state's economic policy. The project had monumental proportions, and expectations mounted as the conference date approached. It was attended by the president and a host of ministers, who displayed an unusual openness to the private sector. Ministers' sectoral-policy presentations were well attended, and dynamic discussions with the audience followed the talks – a novelty in Egypt.

The conference was deemed a resounding success: Egypt received US$12.5bn in assistance from Gulf countries, and signed deals worth US$38.2bn, in addition to US$92bn in memoranda of understanding for future deals. Much of the support came from Gulf countries and Gulf-based companies, reflecting a political investment in the Sisi government. The government also signed lucrative contracts with global firms, such as a US$9bn deal with Siemens, the largest in the company's history.[26] Most importantly, the Egyptian private sector looked on the EEDC very positively, providing a long-awaited, albeit cautious, note of optimism after years of disappointing performance and outlooks. Egyptian investors at the conference were optimistic, albeit cautiously so, and had little doubt that the government would follow up on its pledges.

The flagship event at the EEDC was the unveiling of the government's new five-year macroeconomic framework and strategy for 2014/15–2018/19.[27] An optimistic medium-term plan, developed largely by external consultants, the strategy (or 'Strat_EGY', as it says on the cover, probably a consultant's attempt at humour) lists a plan for restoring macroeconomic stability and supporting growth. Besides structural reforms to strengthen the investment climate, the strategy includes plans for fiscal consolidation; tax and public-spending reforms, particularly in relation to energy subsidies, wages and public financial management, which respectively comprised 22%, 26% and 25% of total expenditures in 2013/14; reduction of public debt from 95.5% to 80–85% of GDP; a deflationary monetary policy to bring inflation down from 11.5% to 6–8% in the medium term; and, finally, an export-promotion strategy. The push to promote exports would mean attracting foreign direct investment, developing free-trade agreements, and shifting towards higher-value-added exports.

The army's economy

Despite the business-friendly rhetoric, Sisinomics has not weakened the army's untouchable economic reach; rather, it has allowed it to flourish and gain new ground. Usually estimated to represent 30–40% of GDP, the army's economic interests date back to the post-colonial era, with President Gamal Abdel Nasser instituting import substitution and public-sector manufacturing policies as early as the 1950s. The army does not publicly acknowledge the magnitude of its involvement in the economy. The head of its department of financial affairs and the most senior officer handling its economic interests have challenged such claims, estimating the value of the army's civilian businesses at around US$1.75bn – less than 1% of the country's GDP.[28] Sisi put the figure at 2%. The role of the army in the economy shows no sign of diminishing – quite the opposite. The army has further consolidated its economic interests since 2013. In September, Adly Mansour, the acting president, issued a decree amending government-procurement legislation, which allowed the state to award government contracts directly to the contractor of its choice in cases of emergency, thus circumventing existing rules and regulations. Following this decree, the army secured contracts worth US$1bn[29] for projects that included bridges and tunnels, housing and a slum-rehabilitation effort – none of which could be considered emergencies.

General Emad el-Alfy, chief of the Armed Forces Engineering corps, has disclosed that, since August 2012, the army has been entrusted with 1,350 development projects, 558 of which have been completed, including in transportation, health, education, water provision and housing. The same corps is involved in the implementation of three major national projects: the New Suez Canal, an extensive road network and the reclamation of one million *feddans*[30] of land. Estimates of the size of the army's real-estate holdings can be gleaned from some of its contracts, but their true extent is unknown. In March 2014, for example, the army announced it was donating land to construct 1m housing units across the country in a billion-dollar deal with Emirati developer Arabtec.[31] The deal is just one of many agreements and joint ventures that the army has regularly participated in, gaining access to global supply chains across a number of industries, including those for automobiles, durable goods and solar panels.[32] This suggests that it is willing to collaborate with other actors, despite maintaining its economic fortress.

The army is cementing its influence in the Egyptian economy and is unlikely to cede any control in the foreseeable future. And this untouchable status is well understood by investors and economic agents, be they local or foreign. Private companies are well aware that it is not advisable to infringe on areas of economic interest to the military. While the army may tolerate competition in certain fields, such as food products, where its markets are primarily within the army itself, firms have learned to conduct their business in parallel with the army, in a stable unspoken arrangement.

Insufficient social-justice and economic-inclusiveness efforts

Most of the population has chosen to trust Sisi and the army's economy. The idea of large-scale projects such as the New

Suez Canal is appealing to the public, especially as they have been presented as a step towards national greatness ('the Great Egyptian Dream') and an assertion of dignity. This may explain why the public appears to have accepted the reduction in fuel subsidies, albeit reluctantly. While lower-income households have expressed discontent, particularly over the increase in the cost of transport, their voices have been absent from the mainstream media. Meanwhile, reactions to Sisi's pro-investment laws have been less sanguine because they are perceived as having little to do with general welfare. Many of the government's business-friendly reforms contradict Sisi's social-justice narrative. For instance, the decision to reverse progressive taxation and reduce the tax rate on the highest-income bracket from 30% to 22.5% – a rate that was only raised in July 2014 – is at odds with government promises to increase social spending because the move limits the state's tax revenues. Demonstrations of support for social justice have been limited to smaller-scale measures, such as the revamping of food-subsidy schemes[33] and the launch of World Bank-supported programmes to enhance social safety nets among the poor.[34] Other examples are a new framework that the central bank has implemented to lend to small- and medium-sized enterprises (SMEs), and the expansion of bank branches to remote areas, with lower capital requirements and a focus on SME lending. However, a key problem with such targeted support programmes is the identification of beneficiaries. In a country with weak registration systems and even weaker poverty-assessment capabilities – notably in the informal, unregistered sector, which is estimated to represent up to 40% of the economy – it is extremely difficult to identify disenfranchised households. Some programmes, such as the 'Social Solidarity' cash-transfer programme, seek to target vulnerable people, such as senior citizens, orphans, widows and divorcees.

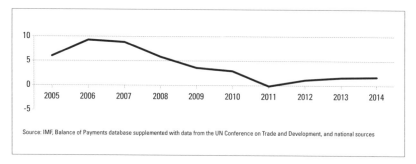

Source: IMF, Balance of Payments database supplemented with data from the UN Conference on Trade and Development, and national sources

Figure 3. **Foreign direct investment, net inflows, % of GDP**

But this is a weak approach to addressing economic hardship because many impoverished people fall outside these categories. As it stands, the identification of beneficiaries is largely self-selective, and therefore inefficient, because it supposes that households that need subsidised goods will invest time and effort in queuing for them – and those who can afford to purchase them at market price will not seek to obtain them at the discounted price. This is clearly not a suitable basis for a social-support system, particularly among a population whose patience has been tested time and again. As the government implements further reforms – in the name of attracting investment – the need for proper mitigation measures will increase if the country is to avoid another popular uprising.

Conclusion

In the official policy documents at the EEDC, the government boasted that it had 'embarked on a number of national large-scale projects', with the goal of 'enhancing the competitiveness of the economy, creating employment opportunities and attracting foreign and domestic private investments'.[35] These bold projects and a business-friendly attitude characterise Sisi's economic policies, which seem to acknowledge the pressing need to reverse the tumultuous economic effects of the past four years. At the very least, these policies have succeeded in raising the level of optimism, locally and internationally, although they have mostly capitalised on Sisi's own celebrity-style popularity at home and strong political support in the region.

Although financial assistance from the Gulf states – nearly US$20bn since 2013 – continues to buoy the government, the situation is unsustainable. A real economic recovery is thus necessary. Government spending and mega-projects will prove insufficient for this, and strong private-sector engagement has been slow to arrive. While the fundamentals of political stability remain absent, a wait-and-see attitude dominates the investment outlook.

The government will need to capitalise on the optimism of investors and rating agencies, as well as the public's good-will and willingness to absorb difficult reforms. But Egyptians will not remain patient indefinitely: people will soon demand results, especially as they begin to feel the brunt of austerity and economic reforms that have not been mitigated by social measures. The government must therefore refocus its economic policy on improving people's quality of life in the short and long term, rather than upgrading its military arsenal and embark-ing on a series of mega-projects without conducting feasibility studies or accurate forecasts of the return on investment.

Notes

[1] Joel Benin, 'The Rise of Egypt's Workers', Carnegie Endowment for International Peace, June 2012, http://carnegieendowment.org/files/egypt_labor.pdf.

[2] 'Egypt's Economy: Light, Dark, and Muddle', Economist, 23 June 2011, http://www.economist.com/node/18864693.

[3] See Bruce K. Rutherford, Egypt after Mubarak: Liberalism, Islam, and Democracy in the Arab World (Princeton, NJ: Princeton University Press, 2013), p. xxxiii.

[4] Patrick Werr, 'Egypt Says it Agrees $3 Billion IMF Loan', Reuters, 30 May 2011, http://www.reuters.com/article/2011/05/30/us-egypt-imf-idUSTRE74T1W020110530.

[5] 'Egypt Drops Plans for IMF Loan amid Popular Distrust', BBC, 25 June 2011, http://www.bbc.

co.uk/news/world-middle-east-13914410.

6 Mohamed El Dahshan, 'Where Will the Muslim Brotherhood Take Egypt's Economy?', *Yale Global Review*, 6 February 2012, http://yaleglobal.yale.edu/content/muslim-brotherhood-take-egypts-economy.

7 'Al-Shater Outlines Egyptian Renaissance Project at First Press Conference', Ikhwanweb, 9 April 2012, http://www.ikhwanweb.com/article.php?id=29859.

8 Borzou Daraghi, 'A New Voice for Egyptian Business', *Financial Times*, 8 November 2012, http://www.ft.com/intl/cms/s/0/a9509002-28ee-11e2-b92c-00144feabdco.html#axzz3XoS7A4YD.

9 *Ibid.*

10 'Mubarak Era Tycoons Join Egypt President in China', Ahram Online, 28 August 2012, http://english.ahram.org.eg/News/51477.aspx.

11 Dahlia Kholaif, 'The Egyptian Army's Economic Juggernaut', Al-Jazeera, 5 August 2013, http://www.aljazeera.com/indepth/features/2013/08/20138435433181894.html.

12 Bassem Abo Alabass, 'Egypt's Energy Crisis: Morsi Cites Success, Upper Egyptians Differ', Ahram Online, 8 October 2012, http://english.ahram.org.eg/News/55022.aspx.

13 Heba Saleh, 'Egypt's Power Crisis Worsened by Declining Natural Gas Production', *Financial Times*, 29 May 2013, http://www.ft.com/intl/cms/s/0/82ae9418-c857-11e2-8cb7-00144feab7de.html#axzz3XzbnZ92x.

14 Zenobia Azeem, 'Egypt's Gas Shortage Fuels June 30 Protests',

Al-Monitor, 27 June 2013, http://www.al-monitor.com/pulse/originals/2013/06/egypt-gas-shortage.html#.

15 'Egypt Unlikely to Seek IMF Loan Before 2014: Future Planning Minister', Ahram Online, 15 July 2013, http://english.ahram.org.eg/NewsContent/3/12/76516/Business/Economy/Egypt-unlikely-to-seek-IMF-loan-before--Future-pla.aspx.

16 Mohamed El Dahshan, 'Does General Sisi Have a Plan for Egypt's Economy?', *Foreign Policy*, 18 April 2014, http://foreignpolicy.com/2014/04/18/does-general-sisi-have-a-plan-for-egypts-economy/.

17 'Al-Sisi's Electoral Platform Proposes New Administrative, Investment Maps', *Daily News Egypt*, 20 May 2014, http://www.dailynewsegypt.com/2014/05/20/al-sisis-electoral-platform-proposes-new-administrative-investment-maps/.

18 'Minister: Egypt Sees Suez Canal Zone Making Up 30–35% of Economy', *Egypt Independent*, 5 March 2015, http://www.egyptindependent.com//news/minister-egypt-sees-suez-canal-zone-making-30-35-economy.

19 See the official website of the Suez Canal Zone at http://www.sczone.com.eg.

20 Sara Aggour, 'Personal Savings Dominate Suez Canal Certificates' Purchases: Baseera', *Daily News Egypt*, 27 September 2014, http://www.dailynewsegypt.com/2014/09/27/personal-savings-dominate-suez-canal-certificates-purchases-baseera/.

21 Ayah Aman, 'Questions Remain on Egypt's Suez Canal Project',

Al-Monitor, 26 August 2014, http://www.al-monitor.com/pulse/originals/2014/08/egypt-sisi-project-new-canal-suez-feasible-economy.html.

22 World Economic Forum, 'Egypt in the World', http://www.weforum.org/sessions/summary/egypt-world.

23 'Egypt's Government Raises Fuel Prices', Ahram Online, 5 July 2014, http://english.ahram.org.eg/NewsContent/3/12/105481/Business/Economy/Egypts-government-raises-fuel-prices.aspx.

24 Heba Saleh, 'Egypt Cuts Spending on Energy Subsidies by a Third in New Budget', *Financial Times*, 30 June 2014, http://www.ft.com/intl/cms/s/0/9da3cb08-007d-11e4-a3f2-00144feab7de.html#axzz3Y6Bh1POY.

25 'Explorers See Promise in Egypt Energy When Subsidies Eased', Bloomberg, 30 June 2014, http://www.bloomberg.com/news/articles/2014-06-30/explorers-see-promise-in-egypt-oil-and-gas-when-subsidies-eased.

26 Archibald Preuschat, 'Siemens Signs $9 Billion Power-Plant Deal With Egypt', *Wall Street Journal*, 3 June 2015, http://www.wsj.com/articles/siemens-signs-9-billion-power-plant-deal-with-egypt-1433343667.

27 Government of Egypt, 'Strat_EGY: Egypt's Five Year Macroeconomic Framework and Strategy, FY 14/15–FY 18/19', available at http://www.egyptthefuture.com/wp-content/uploads/2015/03/EEDC-Strategy-Book-A4-with-cover.pdf.

28 Heba Saleh, 'Egyptian Army's Role Expands as it Gives Land for Homes', *Financial Times*, 23 March 2014, http://www.ft.com/intl/cms/s/0/3b6e0762-b02f-11e3-b0d0-00144feab7de.html#axzz3VdPmxmnE.

29 'The Army Obtains 7 Billion Pounds Worth of Government Construction Contracts in a Month', *Masrawy*, 23 November 2013, http://web.archive.org/web/20131127012531/http://www.masrawy.com/news/Egypt/Economy/2013/November/24/5766489.aspx.

30 A *feddan* is a unit of measurement equivalent to 1.038 acres.

31 Saleh, 'Egyptian Army's Role Expands as it Gives Land for Homes'.

32 Shana Marshall, 'The Egyptian Armed Forces and the Remaking of an Economic Empire', Carnegie Middle East Center, April 2015, available at http://carnegie-mec.org/2015/04/15/egyptian-armed-forces-and-remaking-of-economic-empire.

33 Government of Egypt, 'Strat_EGY'.

34 World Bank, 'US$400 Million Program to Support 1.5 Million Poor Egyptian Families through Enhanced Social Safety Nets', 10 April 2015, http://www.worldbank.org/en/news/press-release/2015/04/10/us400-million-program-to-support-15-million-poor-egyptian-families-through-enhanced-social-safety-nets.

35 EEDC, 'Invest', https://www.egyptthefuture.com/egypt-economic-development-conference-eedc/invest/.

INDEX

Adelphi books are published eight times a year by Routledge Journals, an imprint of Taylor & Francis, 4 Park Square, Milton Park, Abingdon, Oxfordshire OX14 4RN, UK.

A subscription to the institution print edition, ISSN 1944-5571, includes free access for any number of concurrent users across a local area network to the online edition, ISSN 1944-558X. Taylor & Francis has a flexible approach to subscriptions enabling us to match individual libraries' requirements. This journal is available via a traditional institutional subscription (either print with free online access, or online-only at a discount) or as part of the Strategic, Defence and Security Studies subject package or Strategic, Defence and Security Studies full text package. For more information on our sales packages please visit www.tandfonline.com/librarians_pricinginfo_journals.

2016 Annual Adelphi Subscription Rates			
Institution	£651	$1,144 USD	€965
Individual	£230	$393 USD	€314
Online only	£570	$1,001 USD	€844

Dollar rates apply to subscribers outside Europe. Euro rates apply to all subscribers in Europe except the UK and the Republic of Ireland where the pound sterling price applies. All subscriptions are payable in advance and all rates include postage. Journals are sent by air to the USA, Canada, Mexico, India, Japan and Australasia. Subscriptions are entered on an annual basis, i.e. January to December. Payment may be made by sterling cheque, dollar cheque, international money order, National Giro, or credit card (Amex, Visa, Mastercard).

For a complete and up-to-date guide to Taylor & Francis journals and books publishing programmes, and details of advertising in our journals, visit our website: http://www.tandfonline.com.

Ordering information:
USA/Canada: Taylor & Francis Inc., Journals Department, 325 Chestnut Street, 8th Floor, Philadelphia, PA 19106, USA. UK/Europe/Rest of World: Routledge Journals, T&F Customer Services, T&F Informa UK Ltd., Sheepen Place, Colchester, Essex, CO3 3LP, UK.

Advertising enquiries to:
USA/Canada: The Advertising Manager, Taylor & Francis Inc., 325 Chestnut Street, 8th Floor, Philadelphia, PA 19106, USA. Tel: +1 (800) 354 1420. Fax: +1 (215) 625 2940. UK/Europe/Rest of World: The Advertising Manager, Routledge Journals, Taylor & Francis, 4 Park Square, Milton Park, Abingdon, Oxfordshire OX14 4RN, UK. Tel: +44 (0) 20 7017 6000. Fax: +44 (0) 20 7017 6336.

The print edition of this journal is printed on ANSI conforming acid-free paper by Bell & Bain, Glasgow, UK.